"*The Agoraphobia Workbook* provides an excellent source of user-friendly, state-of-the-art guidance on how to overcome one's fears and phobias."

—Richard J. McNally, Ph.D., Professor of Psychology,
Harvard University, author of *Remembering Trauma*

"*The Agoraphobia Workbook* teaches the steps to overcome agoraphobia. This welcome book looks at forms of agoraphobia beyond panic disorder. It is an important new resource for many agoraphobia sufferers who, until now, have been largely ignored by prior authors. This book can also be used by therapists who want to use state-of-the-art procedures with their agoraphobic clients."

—Robert G. Meyer, Ph.D., ABPP, Professor of Psychology,
University of Louisville, author of *The Clinician's Handbook*

THE
Agoraphobia
WORKBOOK

A Comprehensive Program to End Your Fear of Symptom Attacks

C. Alec Pollard, Ph.D. & Elke Zuercher-White, Ph.D.

New Harbinger Publications, Inc.

Publisher's Note

This publication is designed to provide accurate and authoritative information in regard to the subject matter covered. It is sold with the understanding that the publisher is not engaged in rendering psychological, financial, legal, or other professional services. If expert assistance or counseling is needed, the services of a competent professional should be sought.

Diagnostic criteria for panic attack were adapted with permission from the *Diagnostic and Statistical Manual of Mental Disorders, Fourth Edition, Test Revision*. Copyright 2000 American Psychiatric Association.

Distributed in Canada by Raincoast Books

Copyright © 2003 by C. Alec Pollard, and Elke Zuercher-White
          New Harbinger Publications, Inc.
          5674 Shattuck Avenue
          Oakland, CA 94609

Cover design by Poulson/Gluck
Edited by Brady Kahn
Text design by Tracy Marie Carlson

ISBN-10 1-57224-323-6
ISBN-13 978-1-57224-323-1

All Rights Reserved

Printed in the United States of America

New Harbinger Publications' website address: www.newharbinger.com

11   10   09

10   9   8   7   6   5   4   3   2

To Heidi, Matt, and Chloe (CAP)

and

To Raja Zürcher and Valve Org (EZW)

This book is dedicated to you.

Contents

PART 1
What You Need to Know

PART 2
What You Need to Do

PART 3
Evaluating and Continuing Your Progress

We would like to recognize the many people who contributed to this book in one way or another. We begin by thanking our clients, the people who have taught us the most. Their courage and dedication to recovery inspire us to live our lives without surrendering to avoidance. And to those of you who are about to work with this book, we acknowledge your courage and dedication as well.

I (CAP) also want to thank my coworkers for helping me think creatively about clinical problems and for encouraging me to share my ideas with others. I'm especially grateful to my current Anxiety Disorders Center colleagues: Gary Mitchell, MSW, LCSW; Jeanne Kehlenbrink, RN, LPC; Reed Simpson, M.D.; Teresa Flynn, Ph.D.; Susan Englund, Ph.D.; Susan Mojeske, Ph.D.; Erikalin Ashton, Psy.D.; Heidi Pollard, RN, MSN; and all the trainees and other clinical staff members, past and present, from whom I have had the opportunity to learn. Thank you Paula Eslich for your daily assistance and for all you do to help clients get the care they need. I would also like to acknowledge Ronald Margolis, Ph.D., Mark Mengel, M.D., and Craig Nuckles. Without their administrative leadership and support, my work on this book would not have been possible. And I am indebted to my parents, Twila and Alec Sr., whose sense of fairness and respect for all human beings helped prepare me to become a clinician.

I (EZW) am indebted to my mother Raja Zürcher and aunt Valve Org who courageously struggle with their advanced age. Their legacy from Estonia, a small country that was ravaged by foreign occupation over centuries, is education. You can lose everything except what you have learned. The legacy from my father's Swiss-German side, reflected in my cousins Albrecht Schwarz and his wife Rita, Martin Schwarz and his wife Brigitte, Marianne Schrader, and the now deceased Marianne Kemmer and her husband Arnold, is heartfelt openness and hospitality—their gracious *Gastfreundschaft*.

We would both like to thank Brady Kahn for her invaluable editorial contributions and everyone at New Harbinger for helping make this book possible. We also extend our gratitude to Reed Simpson, M.D., William Richardson, M.D., and Heidi Pollard, RN, MSN, for their input regarding the medical information contained in this book. Last but not least, we thank all of our family and friends who tolerated our frequent inaccessibility and erratic schedules during the writing of this book.

Introduction

Do you avoid walking outside alone for fear of feeling dizzy? Do you avoid driving on the freeway because you fear you might faint? Do you fear suddenly having to go to the bathroom in the middle of a movie and being too embarrassed to stand up and leave? Do you fear being too far from home because you might be unable to cope with a headache? Do you avoid going to restaurants because you're afraid you might throw up or lose control of your bowels? If you answered yes to any of these questions, this book may be for you!

We have written this book for people who suffer from agoraphobia. The questions above describe some of the more common manifestations of agoraphobia, but this potentially disabling disorder takes many other forms. What all people with agoraphobia have in common is the fear of having a symptom attack, a sudden, intense rush of one or more internal sensations or physical symptoms, such as vomiting, headaches, or fainting. If you are unsure if this book is for you, please read further. You may be able to benefit from the program we have developed.

Common Misconceptions about Agoraphobia

Many people believe that being agoraphobic means you are unable to leave your home. This or other misconceptions may have led you to conclude that you don't have agoraphobia. Read further and see if any of these misconceptions reflect your understanding of agoraphobia:

All people with agoraphobia are housebound. Being housebound is the most severe form of agoraphobia. In fact, only a minority of people with agoraphobia are housebound. Many people have mild symptoms.

Agoraphobia is a fear of crowds. While some people with agoraphobia fear crowds, others prefer them. Some people with agoraphobia feel that being around others provides a certain degree of safety.

It's not agoraphobia if you just need someone to come along. If you need someone to be with you, even if you can do everything you like, you still can have severe agoraphobia. Relying on someone else for the rest of your life is a restriction imposed by fear. It leaves you dependent on others.

Agoraphobia is a fear of being alone. Many people with agoraphobia are afraid to be alone, but not everyone is. Some people are more afraid when someone else is around because they are concerned about being embarrassed in front of others.

Fear of enclosed spaces is always claustrophobia. Claustrophobia is a much more acceptable fear in our culture than agoraphobia. If you think of it, people readily admit to being claustrophobic, while few admit as openly to being agoraphobic. Claustrophobia refers to a fear of being restricted to small spaces, such as elevators or tiny rooms without windows. Some people with agoraphobia are uncomfortable in enclosed spaces, but usually they have other fears as well. Because the experience often involves fear of the same sensations and catastrophic outcome, *this book may be equally useful if you have claustrophobia* instead of, or in addition to, agoraphobia.

Agoraphobia is a fear of open spaces or public places. It is true that some agoraphobics avoid open spaces or public places, but many do not. When agoraphobics do fear situations, it is because of the threat of experiencing a sudden rush of sensations or symptoms, that is, a symptom attack.

Agoraphobia is a fear of heights. A fear of heights is called *acrophobia,* which sounds similar. Some people with agoraphobia are afraid of high places, but this is rarely the main part of their fear.

Agoraphobia is always a fear of panic attacks. This is not actually the case. People can fear many kinds of symptom attacks. Common to all cases of agoraphobia is the belief that a symptom attack will lead to some catastrophic outcome.

If you have agoraphobia, you may fear a number of situations, but no matter what the situation, your fear always involves *feeling or expecting to feel* something disturbing in those situations. You think you cannot handle or cope with certain sensations, which you believe could have terrible consequences. Most people with agoraphobia have not truly experienced the ultimate catastrophe they fear. They may have experienced distress or embarrassment, but no catastrophe has ever actually occurred.

Though no two cases of agoraphobia are identical, there are some common aspects to agoraphobic fears. It may help you to hear about one person's experience with agoraphobia. Here is how Ann's agoraphobia began:

Ann is going through a nasty divorce. It causes a great deal of anxiety and anger, creating a negative state of anxious arousal. Then, one day while in the mall, Ann feels sick, as if she is going to throw up. She finds a bathroom and throws up. She is relieved to have reached the bathroom in time. Yet the next time she finds herself in a crowded grocery store, standing in a long line and feeling just a little strange in the stomach, she wonders if she will get nauseated. The line seems to take forever and she wonders what would happen if she needed to throw up. She suddenly experiences an intense anxiety attack.

Why would this happen to her? We know Ann is currently more anxious than usual, she might have a biological predisposition to anxiety, and on top of it, Ann, whose life is falling apart because of the divorce, is desperately trying to keep control over herself and her life. The initial vomiting episode might have been brought on by a number of circumstances and is not the problem in itself. Ann exaggerates the episode with thoughts such as, "What if I throw up in front of others? They'll find it so disgusting that they'll run from me or think I'm weird!" She starts to worry about where she might throw up next and looks for signs of nausea in situations where she does not have immediate access to the bathroom. To Ann, these situations now signal danger, and she starts to avoid them. She has developed agoraphobia.

Similarly, your thoughts are likely to make a situation worse. With agoraphobia, thoughts create distortions, exaggerating the impact of what might happen. This can occur because your internal alarm system is flexible enough to let you learn to avoid new sources of danger. This flexibility is important for survival. In situations like Ann's, however, the danger is not life threatening.

When You Know Your Fear Is Irrational

Perhaps you already have good insight into your fears, knowing exactly why you fear a certain situation or sensation and that logically it does not make sense. Nevertheless, you cannot help it. You cannot make the fear go away with logic and reasoning. Why?

Dr. Seymour Epstein (1993) explained why in his book, *You're Smarter Than You Think*. We process information in two ways: experientially and rationally. Our behavior results from both modes operating and interacting closely together. Our *experiential mode* is based on early life experiences and beliefs, from which we make generalizations. This is an automatic, adaptive, and smart way of processing information. But the experiential mode sometimes contains unhelpful elements such as irrational fears. These fears are not based on objective reality but rather on how we *interpret* events and information. In contrast, our *rational mode* is comparatively detailed and analytical, depending on language and logical thinking, and capable of abstract thought. But the rational mind has difficulty influencing thoughts based on emotional processing, that is, the experiential mode.

How does this translate to your phobia and how can you change it? The rational and experiential parts of the mind learn differently and are not always in harmony. That is why you can feel you are in danger while another part of you thinks you are safe. Many of our clients have great difficulty resolving these two aspects of their minds. Failure of the rational mind to make the fear go away can be demoralizing. Some people begin to question their intelligence or strength of character, assuming they should be able to talk themselves out of their fear. They don't realize that phobias come largely from the experiential mind, a part of the mind that does not change by logical persuasion. Even geniuses cannot talk themselves out of a phobia.

Overcoming a phobia ultimately requires a change in your thoughts and beliefs, which means both your rational and experiential mind must participate. It is important to examine the rationality of your fear and to learn as much as you can about how dangerous the things you fear truly are. Yet the most powerful learning occurs through direct experience, or *exposure*. When you face and confront something fearful, your emotional mind will react with anxiety and fear, but when you stay with it long enough and realize the dreaded catastrophe does not occur, your brain goes, "Aha! I thought this terrible thing was going to happen and it did not." When you keep repeating the task, habituation takes place. As you get used to the situation, your physical reaction and your psychological experience of fear diminishes, sometimes rather quickly. Your self-confidence rises, and over time you learn to react differently in the same situation. Experience teaches your emotional mind in a way that information and facts cannot. Without the right kind of experiences, your fear is not likely to go away.

Can You Do This on Your Own?

Some people do overcome their phobias without professional assistance. We've heard people say, "I overcame the fear; I just started *doing* things," or, "I just couldn't live that way anymore, so I confronted my fear, little by little." We don't know exactly how many people overcome phobias on their own because those who are successful do not end up in our clinics. We do know that to be successful you have to work hard. Agoraphobia rarely goes away by itself.

If you are trying to address your agoraphobia on your own, this book will teach you how to work with your thoughts and feelings and behaviors. We use the steps of cognitive behavioral therapy (CBT), a method used by knowledgeable therapists to help people overcome their fears. This book is thus a self-help program. It is not a book just to be read. The steps must be learned and practiced diligently. If used properly, they can produce profound changes in you, but you must do two things:

1. Develop a structure and find the discipline to follow it. This involves motivation, time, and effort.

2. Do things that will at times be uncomfortable.

If you find yourself struggling too much or you don't see the progress you'd hoped for, don't hesitate to seek professional assistance. We've worked with a great number of clients with varying types and degrees of agoraphobia and know how hard it can be to overcome it, having observed their struggles. One advantage of a therapeutic setting is that the therapist can guide you through the stages of recovery and help you deal with obstacles as they arise. Your therapist can follow the steps of this book along with you. If you do seek professional help, try to find a therapist who practices CBT.

Now back to your task. Take heart! Imagine us standing by and leading and cheering you along. We have great empathy for you and have confidence in your ability to make these changes in your life.

Why We Wrote This Book

Both of us have been treating agoraphobia and other anxiety disorders for many years. When we first began in this field, most people, including health-care professionals, knew very little about agoraphobia. Since then, things have changed for the better. People with agoraphobia and professionals who treat it have appeared numerous times on *Oprah* and other talk shows. The National Institute of Mental Health, the Anxiety Disorders Association of America, and other organizations have conducted national campaigns to educate the general public about agoraphobia and other anxiety disorders. Today the average person is better informed about this disorder than ever before. So why did we feel it was necessary to write a book on agoraphobia at this time?

We had several reasons. Most books on agoraphobia were written a number of years ago, and some of the information they provide is outdated. Books on panic disorder tend to be more contemporary, but they focus exclusively on agoraphobia associated with fear of panic attacks and do not cover the many other types of fears people can experience. We are unaware of any book for consumers that adequately addresses agoraphobic fears of other symptom attacks, such as vomiting, headache, or loss of bladder or bowel control. We felt there was a need for a comprehensive book covering all forms of agoraphobia. Finally, we believed there was a need for an agoraphobia workbook that provides more structure and guidance than that typically provided by other self-help books on agoraphobia.

How to Use This Workbook

This book consists of three parts. In part 1, you will learn more about your phobia and why it has not gone away. In part 2, you will proceed with the steps to overcome your agoraphobia. Part 3 will help you with any difficulties you may encounter.

If you choose to try the program outlined in this book, you will find that we provide a great deal of guidance. This book is based on what we know works. You may choose to modify our approach, but be careful. Remember that your way has not worked in the past. Shortcuts usually do not lead to a good outcome. *Please try to follow the steps we suggest.* If it turns out to be too difficult, seek professional help.

Since this is a workbook, we ask you to use a pad and pen as you proceed through the book. Underline and highlight sections you find particularly relevant or important. Take notes, written in your own words. Writing something in addition to reading it, saying it out loud, and talking to others about it makes learning much more complete. Do things in order. The worksheets build upon one another. If you skip one or more, you may be skipping an essential part of the program. That is why it is important to do them all in sequence.

Before going on to chapter 1, please refer to appendix F. There you will find the worksheets that make up such a large part of the program. Go ahead and copy them before you get more involved in the book. Be sure to also read the text that appears on the first page of appendix F. Then delve into chapter 1. We also urge you to read the chapter summaries at the beginning of each chapter to have a good grasp of what is involved in the program.

It is now time to proceed with your recovery. Good luck!

PART 1

What You Need to Know

In part 1, we will provide the information you need to know before taking active steps to overcome your agoraphobia. You'll learn about the nature of fears and phobias in general and agoraphobia in particular. We'll discuss why your agoraphobia has not disappeared and why you need to take a new approach. Finally, we'll cover the common pitfalls you might encounter along the way and how to maximize your chances for recovery.

1

Understanding Fears and Phobias

Where We're Going

In this chapter, you will learn why we as humans experience fear and anxiety. Although the material gets a bit technical, it will help you understand what anxiety symptoms are all about, the useful purpose they can serve, and why they won't harm you. You will also see how easily a phobia can develop—not always as the result of a major trauma. One of us will share her own confrontation with a phobia and you will learn some phrases that have inspired other people to face the things they fear.

Fear and anxiety are the natural alarm system, found in humans and many animals. They are designed to warn us of potential danger. Over aeons, a defense system has evolved to cope with danger in order to ensure our survival. When threatened, the *fight/flight response* gets triggered. This hard-wired response is largely automatic. In other words, it is a reflex that occurs whether or not we want it to. As the words indicate, we will either fight to defend ourselves or try to escape.

When fear is activated, there are three components to the response. These fear-response systems are

- *physiological changes* that quickly produce strength to fight or flee

- *thoughts* of impending doom, accompanied by an emotional state of fear and anger

- *behaviors* which consist of fighting and/or fleeing

The Physiology of Fear

When threat registers, fear activates the hypothalamus in the brain, and a signal is sent to the *autonomic nervous system.* This is a part of the nervous system that functions automatically, or outside of awareness. It is responsible for the regulation of respiration, circulation, digestion, body temperature, and so on. The autonomic nervous system consists of two main parts: the *sympathetic nervous system* (SNS) and the *parasympathetic nervous system* (PNS). The SNS is responsible for mobilizing the body and preparing it for the fight/flight response. The PNS relaxes the body and brings it back to normal. These two systems help maintain the body's balance. Hence, we need both.

In the fight/flight response, many changes take place. Fear activates the SNS as an entire unit producing a *mass discharge.* This reaction results in the following changes:

- *Cardiovascular:* The heart starts beating faster and harder; its job is to redistribute the blood to help deliver oxygen and glucose where it is needed. There is increased blood flow to the big muscles and decreased flow to the skin, hands and feet, gastrointestinal tract, and kidneys. Decreased blood flow to the extremities (hands and feet) produces sensations of numbness, tingling, and cold. When the blood brings extra oxygen and glucose to the arms and legs, the muscles get stronger. This is needed to fight or flee. (Think of the symptoms you experience in a panic, and you will begin to see the connections between panic attacks and the fight/flight response.)

- *Pulmonary:* The lungs respond to the danger signals, and breathing becomes heavier and faster. Again, more oxygen is needed for the muscle tissues.

- *Sweat glands:* Increased sweating helps regulate body temperature and prevents it from rising to dangerous levels.

- *Mental:* The mind gets intensely focused on the threat; it concentrates only on the present danger. This means that you do not worry about irrelevant matters, such as whether you left dirty dishes in the sink. The emotions you experience are fear and/or anger.

- *Behavioral:* The behavior consists of fighting or fleeing. Fighting is associated with a mental state of anger. Fleeing is associated with a mental state of fear.

- *Other effects:* The pupils will dilate to increase the visual field, the blood coagulates faster to protect against hemorrhage, and increased blood pressure improves circulation.

The adrenal glands release *adrenaline* and *noradrenaline* into the blood stream. These chemicals also help prepare the body for the fight/flight response, just as the SNS does. They help sustain the activity for a while, in case the danger returns. You may wonder what would happen if the SNS or adrenaline and noradrenaline maintained the arousal state indefinitely. This would be very dangerous, indeed, but, in fact, when the body has had enough, balance is restored. First, the PNS automatically kicks in to counteract the activity of the SNS. Second, adrenaline and noradrenaline are destroyed by other chemicals released into the bloodstream. Nature would hardly create such an elaborate protective mechanism if it killed you in the process! (For more information on why some people develop panic and phobias and on differences between fear and panic symptoms, see appendix A.)

True Alarms and False Alarms

Although sometimes the only option is to fight, fleeing is often more advantageous. Escape moves us away from the danger, and we are strongly compelled to want to escape. Another defensive response, avoidance, is similar, but avoidance occurs in *anticipation of danger*. Both types of response are attempts to protect ourselves.

The fight/flight response allows us to learn to fear potential new threats quickly. This highly reactive system is adaptive because it is better to respond, even if ultimately the situation is not dangerous, than to risk death by not having picked up a possible threat signal. Our danger detection system subscribes to the principle of better safe than sorry. However, that means we can experience false alarms. A false alarm is one that occurs when there is no real danger present. Fight/flight responses in the presence of real danger are called *true alarms;* they are responses to imminent life-threatening danger (Barlow 1988).

Öhman and Mineka (2001) point out that with a more sophisticated nervous system, such as that found in humans, the fear response is less preprogrammed. That is, humans are capable of learning new responses. Things that elicit fear can be vastly expanded through conditioning, such as when neutral (nondangerous) signals are paired with a perceived threat. Humans can associate fear with external situations such as going to shopping malls or with internal sensations such as rapid heartbeat or dizziness. Such new fears can be acquired sometimes even in a single trial. When this happens, these *false alarms* have now become learned.

From False Alarms to Learned Alarms

How does an initial false alarm develop into a learned false alarm? Think of Ann's case, described in the introduction. One requirement is that there exists a heightened state of anxiety or arousal (Ann going through a divorce). This becomes coupled with an aversive event (Ann felt nauseated and threw up). These two elements alone would not have created a phobia. An additional element was her thinking that it would be terrible if she were to throw up in front of others, fearing their disgust toward her. Going back to evolution, primates and humans are biologically predisposed to fear facial expressions of threat, anger, or disapproval. It is thus not surprising that Ann started to worry about people's reactions. This type of biological preparedness in and of itself does not mean a disorder will develop. Psychological factors and stress with arousal are needed for fear to develop. All were present in Ann's situation. Subsequently, she experienced an anxiety attack, which was in fact a false alarm. Nonetheless, she developed a strong association between being in a public place and her fear of vomiting, and her reaction of alarm further reinforced her feeling of dread. She learned to fear and avoid public places where she feared vomiting; it became a *learned alarm* (Barlow 1988). This was the beginning of her agoraphobia.

In a true alarm, the cause of the alarm is usually clear: a dog is charging uncontrollably at you, someone is pointing a gun at you, and so forth. In contrast, the cause of a false alarm is not always clear. As a result, unlike true alarms, false alarms are likely to *generalize* to other situations, meaning they begin to occur in different contexts that may have only a superficial similarity to the original situation (Barlow 1988). As Öhman and Mineka (2001) point out, we can isolate elements within a situation that convey a potential threat and start responding with fear to those elements. (This allows the perceived fear to be quite removed from any real threat.) Going back to Ann, she could become sick anywhere, but she became anxious when she felt stuck around others. Ann concluded there is no easy exit when standing in a long line or being in the upper floors of a department store; she felt trapped in those particular situations. (Do you recognize this thinking in yourself?) Objectively seen, her thinking created a distortion by exaggerating the bad outcome. Her attention became selective and she started to look for every way in which she felt trapped. This response is in contrast with that of the average person, who looks instead for every way he or she is *not* trapped, and thinks, "I can leave the line any time I want." (The average person is not necessarily conscious of this thought in a given situation, but if you were to ask him or her, that would be the response.) You might wonder why the phobic person develops an obsession with entrapment. According to Barlow (1988), when a false alarm occurs in a situation that prevents, even partially, the powerful behavioral tendency to escape, the alarm is further intensified. This results in strong emotional learning.

In the future, when Ann is in one of her agoraphobic situations where she feels trapped, she may respond with fear, even a full-blown panic attack. In this case the panic attack *is secondary to her fear of not being able to get to the bathroom fast enough to throw up.* In other words, she is not afraid of the panic attack. Her panic is a response to the situation. Her fear is of throwing up.

Can Learned Alarms Change?

Fortunately, humans have the capacity to change. You are not doomed to live with your irrational fears indefinitely. If you provide yourself with the right kinds of experiences and approach the situation properly, you can learn new responses, even to things you may have feared for many years. Take Ann, for example. She can choose to practice staying for increasingly longer periods of time in feared situations, combating the impulse to escape. If she does this, Ann will learn that she is not as easily nauseated as she thinks, she does not really tend to throw up, and she will slowly regain confidence. Even if she does throw up (and people do), she will learn she can handle whatever reactions she might encounter.

In the introduction, we said it is difficult to change irrational fears through reasoning alone, the rational mind having only a limited direct impact on the emotional mind. We also said exposure is a superior mode of learning, because exposure directly produces new experiences. Going back to the three fear-response systems (physiological, mental, and behavioral) that we discussed earlier in this chapter, Marks and Dar (2000) point out that the these systems are interconnected; therefore, change in one system can impact the others. We also know from clinical experience that the effects of exposure can be counteracted by unhelpful ways of coping with fear. For instance, if every time you are on the freeway, you say to yourself, "This is awful. It is dangerous. I need to get off. Why did I get on the freeway to begin with?" your thinking might counteract the positive effect of a safe exposure to the freeway because you keep a heightened state of anxiety throughout your drive. In this book's program, you will therefore work on your thoughts and beliefs as well. And you will learn strategies to cope with fear. As you progress in one area, it can have a domino effect on the others. Work in one area facilitates change in the others. As you learn to tolerate your fear-laden thoughts and feelings without reacting, you will gain emotional confidence and not automatically resort to escaping.

Summary of the Previous Sections

To recap the technical sections above:

- Our bodies and minds react to danger by eliciting the fight/flight response. This is designed by nature to *protect*; hence, it will not harm us. Many changes take place in our bodies and minds, all designed to create strength in our behavioral attempts to survive.

- The term "true alarm" refers to when the danger is real, that is, imminently life threatening.

- A false alarm, or panic, is the fight/flight response triggered in the absence of life-threatening danger.

- A learned alarm is when you repeatedly react with fear (including with a panic attack) in a situation that is not dangerous, such as in an elevator or a store or on a bridge. Unwittingly, you start to scan for danger signals where there aren't any.

A Personal Account of Fear

We said that the more powerful way of learning to overcome fears is through the behavioral system. We also said that all three systems (including the physiological and mental) influence each other. Let us indulge in one example of how the mental system (consisting of thoughts and feelings) was the primary system in overcoming a fear. This is what happened to one of us.

Elke used to have a rather intense fear of extreme heights. This fear is common in humans and believed to be partly biologically based. Elke had worked with people with panic and phobias for a number of years. One day, she was discussing fears with colleagues and mentioned that she had a fear of extreme heights, but when she said it, the words did not seem to ring true. Soon thereafter, she attended the conference of the Anxiety Disorders Association of America in Los Angeles. Checking in to her hotel, she asked for a room with a view and got one on the twenty-fifth floor. She was shown to the elevators.

The elevator she entered was crowded, so she faced the elevator door. Soon thereafter, on the second or third floor, the inside of the elevator became very bright. After a while, she heard someone breathing behind her, and she realized that someone was hovering closer to her (and to the door). She guessed that the elevator had windows to the outside, and the person next to her was obviously afraid. Once other people got off, she finally turned around and realized she was in an outside elevator, moving up the wall of the building. Three sides of the elevator were made of glass! Right then and there, she realized she was no longer fearful. Looking straight down along the outer glass, she thought it would be awful to come crashing down, but then, "Why would that happen?" she thought. "We are not in the middle of an earthquake." She stayed on the elevator. Throughout the remainder of the conference, she took many opportunities to use the elevator, always positioning herself by the outer glass and looking straight down. She wanted to assure herself that the fear was indeed gone. Since then, she has accompanied a few clients on this type of elevators in San Francisco.

The change in Elke's fear structure was the result of years of work with clients. On the thinking level, her fear was as irrational as that of her clients, since her life was not in imminent danger. On the emotional level, she had often identified with her clients' fears and accomplishments. While this rapid recovery is not likely to occur when you first confront your fears, it may well happen later. As you conquer some feared situations through hard work, you may be able to make quick improvements in other situations.

Taking a Different Look at Anxiety

If you think of Ann's example and possibly your own, what is striking is how harmlessly it all started. Ann had no idea that going through a divorce would result in agoraphobia. Most likely, this development took place without Ann sharing her initial reaction and her thoughts with a trusted friend. Even her early avoidance seemed natural in order not to feel fear and discomfort. She got caught up in a fear response network that swept her along. We firmly believe many people would not have become agoraphobic had they known more about anxiety and how certain thoughts and behaviors exacerbate it, and had they been able to put their concerns about other people's reactions into perspective. Ann might have been too sensitive to the opinions of others, but she was not terrified of people, and she functioned quite well. Of course, as prevention, she might have benefited from professional or self-help support for the divorce. Like many people going through divorce, she often felt alone, overwhelmed, and fearful of the future. But how could she have known she was vulnerable to developing agoraphobia? She simply struggled along with her divorce as many others do in stressful situations.

Even some basic information about anxiety and phobias could have helped Ann a great deal. Here are some truths about anxiety and fear and some helpful mottos that we suggest you follow. Unfortunately, neither you nor Ann had the benefit of knowing these things before developing agoraphobia, but we hope you can make use of them now.

Truths about Anxiety and Fear

- **Anxiety Is a Part of Life**
  Only the dead are not anxious. The goal should never be to get rid of anxiety completely. Anxiety is necessary for life.

- **Anxiety Does Not Kill**
  Anxiety is there to protect and motivate you.

- **Anxiety and Panic Do Not Last Forever**
  A panic attack has a clear beginning and a clear downturn. Nature has designed ways to protect us from being harmed by prolonged anxiety and panic.

- **Anxiety Is Fear**
  When you think about anxiety, translate it into fear to understand it better. If you are anxious, it means you fear something.

- **Fear Tends to Be Specific**
  Sometimes you might have to struggle to find what makes you anxious (what you fear), but it's almost always there.

- **Anxiety Is Future-Oriented: It Has to Do with Uncertainty**
  You cannot control the uncertainty of the future, but you can try to accept it. In contrast, the past is known. There is no anxiety or worry about the past, unless a past event has unknown repercussions for the future. You may feel regrets about the past, but not anxiety.

- **The Things You Avoid Are Not the Problem**
  It is how you interpret and respond to situations that creates problems.

- **The More Energy You Put into Controlling Anxiety, the Less You Can Control It**
  The paradox is that only when you accept your anxiety will it cease to be a problem.

- **The More You Place Anxiety on a Pedestal, the More of Your Life It Will Take Up**
  If you let it, anxiety will take over more and more of your life. The more you let anxiety dictate your actions, the less freedom you will have.

- **"A Panic Attack Is As Bad As You Fear It at the Time and It Will Last As Long As You Keep Fearing It"**
  This is a wonderful motto to heed. Dr. Roger Tilton said this at the Conference of the Anxiety Disorders Association of America (2000).

- **Many Commonly Feared Physical Symptoms are Intensified by Anxiety**
  A variety of unwanted symptoms can be triggered, intensified, or prolonged by the psychophysiological effects of anxiety. Onset of the symptom will elicit anxiety in someone who fears that symptom.

- **Avoidance Feeds Anxiety**
  You *never* overcome a phobia by avoiding it. Fear is increased in the absence of learning about and facing the situation you fear.

- **Confidence Comes Only on the Other Side of Fear**
  Staying away from anxiety through avoidance, or even through the use of medications, does not give you the experience you need in order to know that you can handle it. Only when you encounter and master phobic situations are you truly free.

Mottos That Can Help You Face Your Fears

- **There Is No Absolute Certainty of Safety**
  Life is risky because as long as we are alive we are at risk of being harmed and dying. Unless you accept the uncertainty of life, you can *always* find something else to fear.

- **The Biggest Wisdom in Life Is Living in the Here and Now**
  To fully immerse yourself in the moment, not thinking about being somewhere else, allows you to live life it its entirety. This is important precisely because you don't know what will happen tomorrow.

- **Being Imperfect Is Humble**
  Striving for perfection creates undue anxiety. It is okay to strive for doing your best. That is the best anyone *can* do. But every human being makes mistakes and you are no different.

- **"We Can't Live the Rest of Our Lives Scared"**
  This was said by a child about flying shortly after September 11, 2001, the day of the terrorist attacks on New York and Washington, D.C. There are no guarantees in life, but you have to go on living.

- **People Are Not As Unforgiving about Your Frailties As You Think They Are**
  Most people will accept others' mistakes and imperfections. When a negative judgment does occur, it is more often a reflection of the person doing the judging than it is of the person being judged.

- **Courage Is Not the Absence of Fear**
  The greatest acts of courage are those performed despite fear. There is nothing more courageous than overcoming your fears.

2

Understanding Agoraphobia

Where We're Going

Now that you know something about anxiety, fear, and phobias, we will focus our attention on agoraphobia in particular. In this chapter, you will learn the unique features of agoraphobia, why it occurs, and who is afflicted by it. You will also learn the different types of agoraphobia and may recognize your own phobia as you read about them. We will once more become a little technical in order to explain why agoraphobia is sometimes hard to recognize, for both laypeople and therapists. Finally, we distinguish agoraphobia from other phobias.

The word *agora* is Greek for "marketplace"; in ancient Greece, the *agora* was an open space, usually in the center of the city, where there were public buildings and religious temples. The word *phobos,* also Greek, means flight, fear, or dread. The term "agoraphobia" was used for the first time in a clinical context in 1871 by the German physician Carl Friedrich Westphal (1988). Westphal saw a number of patients who feared walking through open spaces or empty streets, going to church or entering other large rooms of people, or riding in trains. His patients also described strong sensations of anxiety, even terror. Westphal used the word "agoraphobia" to mean a fear of spaces.

Over time, "phobia" has come to mean an irrational fear that is excessive to a given situation, leading to avoidance of a feared event or place. In the last couple of decades, agoraphobia has become associated largely with a syndrome known as *panic disorder.* A number of people with agoraphobia have unexpected panic attacks and then start to fear having them, which often brings on more attacks. Ultimately, they begin avoiding a number of situations for fear of having a full-blown panic attack. Panic-related agoraphobia has received a great deal of attention from researchers and theoreticians. However, as you will soon discover, there are many other types of agoraphobia.

Formal Definitions and Diagnostic Issues

The latest edition of the *Diagnostic and Statistical Manual of Mental Disorders (DSM-IV)* (American Psychiatric Association 2000) defines agoraphobia as anxiety about being in places or situations from which escape may be difficult because of physical or social constraints (embarrassment) or where help may not be available in the event of a panic attack or panic-like symptoms (such as a sudden attack of dizziness or diarrhea, or loss of bladder control). The symptoms feel incapacitating or embarrassing. As a consequence, agoraphobics avoid doing things outside the home, entering crowded situations, taking public transportation, driving, going in elevators, being home alone, and so on. You either avoid the feared situation or enter it with great discomfort. Being accompanied may allow agoraphobics to do some of the feared activities. Note: If you suffer from an identified medical condition, fear of incapacitation or embarrassment must be clearly excessive to the condition in order to qualify for a diagnosis of agoraphobia.

The *DSM-IV* identifies two types of agoraphobia. One type involves a fear of panic attacks, and is called *panic disorder with agoraphobia* (PDA). The *DSM-IV* defines panic attacks as *sudden* surges of intense fear accompanied by a number (at least four) of the following symptoms: palpitations/pounding heart, sensations of shortness of breath or smothering, light-headedness/dizziness/faint feelings, sweating, hot or cold flushes, trembling/shaking, numbness/tingling, choking sensations, nausea/abdominal distress, chest pain/discomfort, feelings of unreality, fear of dying, and fear of going crazy or losing control. To be diagnosed with PDA, you must experience some panic attacks that seem to come out of the blue, or are not predictably attached to a situation. People with other phobias may have panic attacks when confronted with (or while anticipating) the situations they fear, but the fear of *unexpected* panic attacks is a central feature of PDA.

The second type of agoraphobia is *agoraphobia without history of panic disorder* (AWHPD). This diagnosis is a mixed category that includes fear of any symptom attack other than panic. People with phobias related to a fear of vomiting or headache, for example, would be classified in this category. Strictly speaking, you must have no history of panic disorder in order to meet criteria for AWHPD, regardless of the type of symptom attack you currently fear.

There are some problems with the *DSM-IV* classification of agoraphobia. First, it is questionable whether the two types of agoraphobia should be separated. The various forms of agoraphobia have more similarities than differences. We will discuss these common elements of agoraphobic fear in the next chapter. Second, because the AWHPD category requires *no history* of panic disorder, you will be assigned a PDA diagnosis if you have had unexpected panic attacks in the past, whether or not you suffer from them now. Consider a forty-two-year-old man who avoids driving alone for fear of having an unexpected migraine headache. Let's say ten years ago he had panic disorder. Even though he does not currently fear panic attacks, technically he would be diagnosed with PDA. This criterion ignores what a person truly fears.

These problems are not present in the *International Classification of Diseases and Related Health Problems (ICD-10)* (World Health Organization 1992). The *ICD-10* distinguishes between *anxiety states*, which include panic attacks and panic disorder, and *phobic states*, which include agoraphobia and other phobias. You might then be diagnosed with a phobic state alone or also an anxiety state (such as panic disorder). Agoraphobia can thus stand on its own without having to be associated with panic disorder. In the *ICD-10*, no distinction is made based on the type of symptom attack the individual fears.

How We Define Agoraphobia

In this book, we will deviate a little bit from the *DSM-IV* classification system and will look at agoraphobia as a diagnostic entity in itself. We see PDA and AWHPD as belonging to the same category. We think this is a more useful way to understand agoraphobia and justify it for two reasons. First, international thinking, as reflected in the *ICD-10,* follows a similar line of thought. Second, the *DSM-IV* is likely to change. It is not an eternal truth but, rather, a work-in-progress with hopefully increasing accuracy. As new research sheds light on this and other disorders, we believe the next edition of the *DSM-IV* will be more consistent with our definition.

Here is our definition of agoraphobia: *Agoraphobia is a maladaptive fear of and desire to avoid situations in which the individual believes a symptom attack may occur and result in incapacitation, humiliation, or some other catastrophe.*

The central theme in agoraphobia is that you fear being somewhere where a symptom attack might occur. Although there are many different symptom attacks feared by people with agoraphobia, the various attacks have some common features. *They all have a sudden and rapid onset and are perceived as unpredictable and uncontrollable.* In almost every case, the feared symptom attack is perceived as leading to catastrophe. These feared catastrophic consequences include death, insanity, loss of control, and humiliation (Pollard et al. 1996). Phobic avoidance may be limited to a certain situation, or it can expand to many other situations—wherever the individual believes symptom attacks might occur.

What Causes Agoraphobia and How Common Is It?

No single cause has been identified that can explain all cases of agoraphobia. Most experts believe the disorder is influenced by a combination of factors that may include genetics, biochemical irregularities, stressful life events, learning history, inaccurate beliefs about the danger of bodily symptoms, and other factors. Fortunately, for this self-help program to work, you don't need to know all the factors that might have contributed to your agoraphobia. Even in therapy, knowing the cause of a problem is not usually required for a successful outcome. This is because what originally caused the disorder may no longer be present or relevant to the process of recovery. What you need to know, however, is what maintains your agoraphobia. Successful strategies for eliminating phobias, like cognitive behavioral therapy and the protocol outlined in this book, address the factors that keep a disorder going and teach ways to change it.

According to epidemiological studies, agoraphobia is estimated to affect between 2.8 and 5.7 percent of the population (Barlow 1988). This range may reflect how the studies were conducted and variations in the populations interviewed. With the recent emphasis on panic disorder, agoraphobia without panic disorder has often taken a backseat in research. This is partly because panic attacks often prompt people to seek treatment, whether or not they have agoraphobia. We know that a large percentage of people with agoraphobia do not seek treatment or help. Many cope by avoiding feared situations when they can and enduring them when they can't. In either case, they suffer and the phobias limit their lives: they are not free.

The incidence of panic disorder is somewhat higher in women than men. At least 60 percent of people with panic disorder develop agoraphobia (Klerman 1992). Of those who develop agoraphobia, 75 percent are women. Men tend to resort more often to alcohol and drugs than avoidance to cope with anxiety and panic. These differences between men and women may be influenced by biological factors. However, social factors may play an equally important role. For example, it has been more acceptable for women to stay close to home and not venture out as much, while men have been the bread-winners, who need to go out more often. These and other sex role differences may account for the ways in which men and women cope with fear.

Different Types of Agoraphobia

Now that you know the central themes that unite all forms of agoraphobia, it's important to learn the different types of symptom attack individuals fear. We will describe some of the more common types of agoraphobia. See if you notice your own symptoms in any of the descriptions below.

Agoraphobia with Fear of Panic Attacks

This is probably the most common type of agoraphobia and has certainly been the most widely studied. Given the nature and number of symptoms associated with panic, it is not difficult to understand why so many people misinterpret the symptoms of these attacks as a sign of heart attack, stroke, insanity, or other catastrophe. In addition to external situations like crowds, traveling far from home, and driving, people with this disorder often avoid physical exertion or anything else they perceive might create the symptoms they fear. Multiple emergency room visits are a common and expensive outcome of this type of agoraphobia.

Agoraphobia with Fear of Headaches

No one likes headaches, but some people are afraid of them and think headaches are a sign of serious disease or will lead to disaster. The most obvious feared outcome of headaches is a stroke. However, some people fear psychological or social consequences, like losing control or going crazy. What people avoid, of course, varies from person to person. One woman could not venture more than ten minutes from her home, which was the amount of time between the initial aura (a sensation that precedes migraine headaches) and the onset of her migraine headaches, which she actually experienced about once a year. Home was her safety zone where she felt safe in case she lost her mind from the headache.

Agoraphobia with Fear of Vomiting

Throwing up is another unpleasant, somewhat unpredictable symptom attack that can elicit fear. Some people with this fear are abnormally prone to vomit, but very often they have rarely thrown up and may never have vomited in the situations they are avoiding. There are at least two types of feared outcomes that can be associated with a fear of vomiting. The most common type we see is a fear of being humiliated in front of others. This fear is often accompanied by an avoidance of social situations, especially restaurants. People with this fear often do not care if they throw up at home. The other type of fear is not related to social concerns. Rather, the fear is of the experience of vomiting itself. It does not matter if they are alone or in public. They feel they cannot handle the experience of throwing up. No matter what the feared outcome is, people with a fear of vomiting often restrict their food intake and engage in other avoidant behaviors they believe will prevent nausea. In some cases, this behavior can seriously jeopardize their physical health.

Agoraphobia with Fear of Loss of Bladder or Bowel Control

Some people fear losing urinary or bowel control. In some cases, there is a real problem with bladder or bowel control, possibly due to a medical condition. In most cases, however, physical control is normal but the agoraphobic fears, "what if?" Usually, the feared outcome is humiliation and the avoidance focuses on social situations. Like those who fear vomiting, people with this fear often engage in unhealthy eating habits or abuse medicines in an attempt to control their digestive system.

Agoraphobia with Fear of Fainting

A fear of fainting can be associated with a fear of panic attacks, but some people do not tie the experience of fainting to the experience of panic and are afraid only of passing out. In some cases, there is a medical reason why the person should be concerned about fainting, but more often the person has rarely if ever passed out. Sensations of dizziness, light-headedness, or being off balance are seen as signs of impending loss of consciousness, creating fear whenever they occur. The perceived danger of fainting is sometimes physical harm or death, but very often it has to do with embarrassment. People fear others will judge them as being weak or will ridicule them. Agoraphobic people who fear fainting often take extra precautions (they walk near the wall or sturdy objects, use a cane, or avoid sudden turns or movements) to ensure they won't fall. Those who fear being humiliated or embarrassed will also dread or avoid social situations where others could witness their collapse.

Other Agoraphobic Fears

There are many other types of symptom attacks that can become the object of agoraphobic fear. Examples include acute pain episodes other than head-ache, mild panic responses called *limited symptom attacks*, and unpredictable attacks of emotions other than anxiety, such as anger or sadness. All of these experiences are time limited, intense, highly unpleasant, largely unpredictable and uncontrollable, and can be perceived as potentially catastrophic. These are the key features of symptom attacks associated with agoraphobia.

Agoraphobic Reactions to Medical Conditions

There is one additional group of agoraphobic symptom attacks that should be considered separately. They may have similar features to other feared symptom attacks we have described, but they are potentially dangerous. All the symptom attacks listed before this section, no matter how uncomfortable or painful, are not medically dangerous in themselves. In some cases, however, people severely restrict their lives for fear of experiencing medical events like seizures, asthma attacks, or heart attacks.

Remember, here we are talking about conditions that have been formally diagnosed by a physician, not simply what someone fears could happen. People vulnerable to these types of attacks should be careful and be sure to follow their physician's directives. However, even in these situations, there may be some misperception of danger, and people with medical conditions sometimes engage in avoidance way beyond the cautions prescribed by their doctor. They also may stop participating in activities that are not capable of triggering the feared symptom attack. Does this sound like you? Whether or not you consider your fears agoraphobic, you may benefit from some of the principles used to help people recover from agoraphobia. In such cases, however, close coordination with a physician is warranted. Your physician should be able to help you determine whether the things you avoid are truly dangerous for your medical condition.

From Fear to Phobia

The onset of agoraphobia can be sudden, or it may develop over time. In the first scenario, an initial full-blown panic attack (a false alarm) or other similarly distressing physiological event can seem to occur out of the blue and immediately create the symptoms of fear and avoidance. Other times, people start fearing physical symptoms associated with the initial symptom attack through a process known as *interoceptive conditioning* (Barlow 1988). The term "interoceptive" refers to internal physiological stimuli or sensations. As a result of conditioning, you learn to associate danger with the sensations, and you can also learn to fear external situations that you perceive as increasing the severity of an attack. Hence, an unpredictable and aversive symptom attack that is perceived as dangerous will lead to fear of situations where the symptom attack may occur. Since you perceive the occurrence of the symptom attack as unpredictable and uncontrollable, you may begin to avoid a number of situations, just to be on the safe side. There is often *persistent anticipatory anxiety*; that is, you may become fearful anticipating entering certain situations.

In this early stage of agoraphobia, you begin to develop vigilance toward sensations that may signal the onset of the feared symptom attack. For instance, a sense of queasiness in the stomach may be seen as a prelude to nausea, which you fear will lead to vomiting. This intensely focused attention can actually exacerbate symptoms or even bring them on, especially in situations where you feel trapped. The actual source of the initial sensation does not always matter. For example, if you fear fainting, you may anxiously respond to a light-headed feeling regardless of what originally caused it. The same fear reaction might occur whether the light-headedness was brought on by anxiety, fatigue, hunger, stress, or illness. Once the sensation is believed to be a sign of danger, it can evoke fear under many different conditions.

Panic attacks can affect people in different ways. Sometimes the feared symptom attack is the panic attack itself. However, when the feared symptom attack is, for example, a diarrhea attack, you might panic in anticipation of an attack of diarrhea. In this case, *the panic attack is secondary* and not the object of fear. The main object of fear is still the diarrhea attack. It is just that the anxiety you experience sometimes reaches extreme form, that is, a panic attack. The panic can thus be the object of fear or the panic can be a fear reaction to another type of symptom attack. The *DSM-IV* diagnosis of panic disorder does not make this distinction clear, which has resulted in some confusion regarding the meaning of panic attacks.

The places that evoke fear are not random. Fear, panic, and avoidance occur mostly outside the home, in public places such as streets, stores, work, school, transportation, auditoriums, and crowds. Public places may be perceived as dangerous because they are outside the safety of home (Lelliott et al. 1989).

People with panic disorder who develop agoraphobia commonly have their first panic attack outside the home; this false alarm is likely to become strongly associated with the place it first occurred (Barlow 1988). The initial fears in panic disorder often involve a fear of heart attack, stroke, suffocation, or some other physical calamity. Over time these fears may evolve to a fear of losing control or embarrassing yourself. In other cases, embarrassment is the central theme from the beginning. For instance, it has been found that embarrassment during the first panic attack often leads to agoraphobia (Amering et al. 1997). Two central themes in agoraphobia are fear of being unable to cope with panic and thereby losing control (crying, going crazy) and fear of the social repercussions from anxiety or panic, such as being laughed at, thought of as weird, and causing embarrassment to yourself or others. *The most consistent feared catastrophes in agoraphobia are fear of losing control (sometimes meaning going insane) and social embarrassment.*

Summary of the Previous Sections

We will summarize once more what may have sounded technical to you. It is not important to remember all the technical controversies surrounding the diagnosis of agoraphobia. Simply remember, for our purposes, agoraphobia is a maladaptive fear of and desire to avoid situations in which you believe a symptom attack may occur and result in incapacitation, overwhelming humiliation, or some other catastrophe.

The fear of symptom attacks can occur through conditioning. The symptom attack is perceived as unpredictable and uncontrollable and the person fears it will have dreadful or unacceptable consequences. In many people, agoraphobia becomes associated with a fear of extreme embarrassment or insanity.

Exercise: How Your Agoraphobia Has Evolved

This is a good place to give you a simple task. It pertains to the material we have covered. Give *brief* answers to the questions. If you cannot put down something in a section, don't worry.

1. How did your agoraphobia start? _____

_____

_____

2. What symptoms or symptom attack did you fear when you first developed agoraphobia? _____

_____

_____

3. If you have high anxiety and panic attacks, are they the main source of fear or do they occur because you fear something else? _____

_____

4. What is your main fear in agoraphobic situations now? (Is this different from what you feared when you first developed agoraphobia?) _____

_____

Jill's Story

One of us worked with a woman named Jill in her early forties. Jill was diagnosed with relatively mild agoraphobia with fear of bowel movement (not diarrhea) attacks. Medically, she had a highly reactive gastrointestinal system. Any slight nervousness or anxiety activated her bowels. By the time she came to the clinic, she was quite distraught over her condition, though she lived a rather full life. When leaving home in the morning, especially when her children needed a ride to school, she had to use the rest room at the last minute when the family already was in the car. However, after getting into the car or driving a little, she often needed to return back home (with the family in the car) to use the rest room again. Over the years she had become increasingly tuned in to the immediate availability of a bathroom. For instance, sitting with her husband over a leisurely breakfast on the weekend while reading the paper or conversing, if her husband got up to go to the bathroom, she would immediately have to go (there was only one bathroom in her house), and her husband would yield with no protest. At work, she sat near the door at meetings. If she did leave to have a bowel movement, she would not return. She was embarrassed that if she returned, she might have to go again and leave a second or a third time.

Jill's recovery was slow over a period of one and one-half years (with only a few treatment sessions, since she applied the exposure guidelines well on her own), because her gastrointestinal system had to slowly become less reactive, that is, decondition from any slight feeling of nervousness or uneasiness. Her treatment included: diaphragmatic breathing to help her physically calm down, having her husband agree to always get up from the breakfast table to go to the bathroom whether or not he needed to. This allowed her over time to become less reactive to the immediate availability of the bathroom. She took increasingly longer walks (away from bathrooms). The plan was to make slow but consistent changes in her behavior or her surroundings. We worked on challenging some of her beliefs about danger as well. She learned to accept her bodily functions as normal and realize that people have better things to occupy their minds with than how often she uses the bathroom.

Jill's problem illustrates many of the features of agoraphobia we have been discussing. We hope her success encourages you to continue to work on your recovery. Keep her story in mind as we move to the next chapter. It is an excellent example of the four primary components of agoraphobic fear you'll be learning about in chapter 3.

Distinguishing Agoraphobia from Other Phobias

All phobias involve dread or avoidance. In addition, panic attacks are not exclusive to agoraphobics. People with almost any phobia can have them. But there are some features that distinguish agoraphobia from other phobias. We will discuss how to distinguish agoraphobia from the two other main categories of phobia: *specific phobia* and *social phobia*.

Specific Phobia

In this type of phobia, the fear is limited to one type of situation. People can have a specific phobia related to almost any kind of thing, including heights, enclosed spaces, animals, natural disasters, medical settings, the dark, water, and traveling. Some of these situations are similar to the situations feared by people with agoraphobia. The difference is in the number of situations avoided, the level of overall anxiety, and the focus of the fear. When several or many situations are feared, when the anxiety level is generally high, and when the person fears internal sensations, then they are diagnosed with agoraphobia. In specific phobia, the fears are externalized to the object (such as an airplane crashing). In agoraphobia, the person also fears certain internal sensations when confronted with the object of fear ("What if I lose control and throw up on the plane?"). People with specific phobias can fear internal sensations, but their concern is usually less severe and restricted to a single type of situation. *Some* people with specific phobias can have significant fear of internal sensations as well.

Space Phobia

A type of specific phobia sometimes confused with agoraphobia is *space phobia,* but the two phobias look similar only on the surface. The term "space phobia" is used in two ways. It is sometimes used to denote a fear of walking through open spaces where there is no tangible visual or physical support (Brandt 1996). This can include walking in wide hallways away from the walls. This condition usually develops late in life, with an average age of onset of fifty-five, and is often linked to either a neurological condition or a previous fall (McCaffrey et al. 1990). The neurological impairment may be subtle, involving difficulty integrating visual and spatial cues. The person worries about and exaggerates the risk of falling. Somatic sensations are insignificant. In extreme cases, the person with space phobia becomes housebound.

Space phobia also refers to a fear of outside space or the sky. Space phobics may fear they will somehow float away into space. They typically avoid looking up into the sky, and they stay away from high places, open areas of the outdoors, and other areas with wide-open vistas. As is the case for almost all people with phobias, they know the phobia is irrational, but they experience the fear anyway.

Social Phobia

This phobia, also known as *social anxiety disorder,* involves a fear of being humiliated or embarrassed. People with social phobia may dread or avoid a number of social situations, some of which are also feared by some agoraphobics. And fear of humiliation and embarrassment can occur in agoraphobia as well as in social phobia. In social phobia, however, the fear is brought on exclusively by a social situation, whereas, in agoraphobia, the fear may not be limited to social situations. Furthermore, fear in agoraphobia focuses on the embarrassment that would result from a symptom attack, and does not usually involve apprehension about social situations in general. People with social phobia usually are concerned about appearing or performing in a variety of ways that might result in criticism or the disapproval of others. If you have social phobia and want to try a self-help book, we recommend *Dying of Embarrassment* (Markway et al. 1992).

This book is written for people with agoraphobic fears. However, if you have other phobias, the principles outlined in this book might work for you as well. This is particularly the case if you fear internal sensations and not just external situations. People with claustrophobia have fears that most resemble those of people with agoraphobia.

3

The Four Components
of Agoraphobic Fear

Where We're Going

By now, you know something about fear in general and agoraphobia in particular. In this very important chapter, we hope to give you a deeper understanding of agoraphobia. We will describe the four primary components of agoraphobic fear: (1) external danger signals, (2) internal danger signals, (3) the feared symptom attack, and (4) the feared catastrophe. We will assist you in identifying each of these aspects of your own fear. This knowledge is essential to progress successfully through the steps of this program.

Agoraphobic fear can be thought of as having four primary components. Without an understanding of each of these components and how they relate to one another, it is easy to become confused about the nature of your fear and how to overcome it. The first two components are called danger signals. They are the very real, anxiety-provoking external situations and internal sensations you encounter with discomfort and avoid when possible. The third component, the feared symptom attack, is that intense and unpleasant experience you believe is foreshadowed by the danger signals. The fourth and final component is the feared catastrophe, the disaster you believe will result from the feared symptom attack if it does not subside and you are unable to escape. Unlike danger signals and the feared symptom attack, it is highly unlikely you have actually experienced the catastrophe you fear. Being convinced you had some close calls is not the same as actually experiencing a catastrophe.

First Component: External Danger Signals

External danger signals are the situations, places, or activities that signal danger to you. They are the situations that make you anxious. When you avoid them, it is the most observable manifestation of your fear. External danger signals communicate potential threat because a symptom attack could occur. Presumably, the situation could also make the consequences of the attack more serious than other situations might.

When we talk about confronting feared situations, this includes doing things *alone,* even situations in which people are normally accompanied, such as going to restaurants and movies. For you to be totally free of irrational fears, it is imperative that you be able to go into situations you fear alone. For instance, you might be traveling somewhere and need to eat in a restaurant by yourself, or there is a movie you want to see, but others you know have seen it or are not interested. Being unable to do these activities alone poses a definite limitation in your life.

Most of the time, people are clear about which situations they fear and which ones they don't. However, some individuals have been avoiding things for so long they may no longer be sure. Or they have convinced themselves there is another "rational" reason why they choose not to enter a particular situation. For instance, "The reason I don't attend baseball games is I hate sports. It's not because I'm afraid of crowds." Be sure to be honest with yourself as you evaluate each situation. While it is true that everyone does not like the same things, people often say they do not like something because it is much harder to admit, "I'm afraid." Take parties, for example. Ask yourself, "Do I really not like parties, or do I fear experiencing a symptom attack there? Do I wish I could attend a party without discomfort?" If you're still not sure, don't guess. Take the time to find out. Approach the situation and see what happens. If you get anxious, guess what?

Feared Situations/Places/Activities

Listed below are the situations, places, and activities most commonly feared by people with agoraphobia. As you go over the list, check all the items that apply to you. For each one, ask yourself, "Do I fear and/or avoid engaging in these activities or entering these situations?" At the bottom of the list, add any external danger signals that apply to you but have not been included here. Later, you will refer back to this list as you set your goals and plan your exposures.

Which of the following situations, places, or activities do you fear?

☐ Being far from home

☐ Being far from hospitals

☐ Being home alone

☐ Walking outside in the neighborhood

☐ Walking in streets far from home

☐ Walking across open spaces

☐ Driving on neighborhood streets

☐ Driving on major roads

☐ Driving on freeways or expressways

☐ Driving over bridges

☐ Driving through tunnels

☐ Being stuck in traffic or stop-and-go traffic

☐ Driving to unfamiliar areas, getting lost driving

☐ Being a passenger in a car

☐ Taking public transportation: buses, streetcars, subways

☐ Taking public transportation: long-distance trains, airplanes

☐ Going to supermarkets

☐ Going to shopping malls

☐ Standing in line

☐ Using elevators or escalators

☐ Being in crowded places

☐ Being in cinemas, theaters, auditoriums

☐ Attending meetings at work

☐ Being in classrooms

☐ Going to restaurants

☐ Going to parties and other optional social events

☐ Doing jury duty

☐ Watching exciting movies, sports events

☐ Being in situations that can lead to disagreements or setting limits with others

☐ Doing exercise or physical exertion

☐ Taking saunas

☐ Having nothing to do

☐ Experiencing heat

☐ Drinking caffeinated drinks

☐ Eating in front of others

☐ Other: _____

_____

_____

_____

Second Component: Internal Danger Signals

Internal danger signals are the *feelings or sensations* that signal the possibility of the symptom attack you fear. These are the sensations that make you anxious. Unlike some phobias, agoraphobia has both internal and external danger signals. Yes, external situations may make you anxious, but only if they are accompanied by an internal danger signal ("Dizziness only bothers me when I'm away from home, and I wouldn't be afraid when I'm away from home if I knew I wouldn't get dizzy"). Remember, agoraphobia is a fear of internal sensations in certain external situations. Both types of signals play a role in provoking fear.

Feared Sensations List

Below we have listed the sensations or symptoms that are most commonly feared by people with agoraphobia. As you go over this list, check the items that apply to you. You may experience a variety of sensations, but check off only those that scare you. Even if the sensations occur in the context of a full-blown panic attack, check only the specific sensations in the attack that *scare* you. For instance, heart palpitations and numbness may scare you in a panic, but not the sweating or nausea you experience. In this case, you would only put a check by "heart palpitations" and "numbness." At the end, add any internal danger signals that are not included on the list, since we have not covered all the possibilities. You will be using this list later when you set your goals and plan your exposures.

Which of the following feared sensations do you experience?

- ☐ Heart palpitations

- ☐ Dizziness, light-headedness

- ☐ Faint-like feelings

- ☐ Shortness of breath, difficulty breathing

- ☐ Choking sensations

- ☐ Numbness, tingling

- ☐ Shaking, trembling

- ☐ Twitching

- ☐ Feeling hot

- ☐ Feeling cold

- ☐ Nausea/indigestion

- ☐ Urge to urinate

- ☐ Urge to defecate

- ☐ Constipation

- ☐ Flatulence

- ☐ Hunger

- ☐ Weakness in the legs

☐ Sweating

☐ Blushing

☐ Feeling disoriented

☐ Poor concentration

☐ Fatigue

☐ Feeling dissociated/detached/as if observing yourself from the outside

☐ Having thoughts go a mile a minute without being able to control them

☐ Migraine aura

☐ Tension in muscles

☐ Distortions in vision

☐ Minor pain (indicate where): _____

☐ Sudden motion

☐ Other: _____

_____

_____

_____

Third Component: The Feared Symptom Attack

Danger signals only provoke anxiety to the extent that they are perceived as signaling an impending symptom attack. Flatulence (an internal danger signal), for example, might generate anxiety because the person believes it is a sign of impending diarrhea (the feared symptom attack). Internal sensations can be feared, but ultimately, it all hinges on the feared symptom attack. The feared symptom attack is that intense and sudden rush of symptoms you try so hard to avoid.

Despite the wide range of symptom attacks feared by people with agoraphobia, these disturbing events have some common features. As we have said before, they tend to be unpredictable and uncontrollable. They have a sudden and rapid onset and peak quickly. Perhaps most importantly, the person feels unable to cope. The feared symptom attack is perceived as leading to incapacitation, death, insanity, or some other catastrophe. The person dreads and wants to avoid situations where these symptom attacks could happen because escape is difficult due to physical constraints (such as being in an airplane) or social constraints (suffering embarrassment when leaving a meeting or the movie theater).

Feared Symptom Attacks

Listed below are the most commonly dreaded symptom attacks. As you look them over, check the items that best reflect the symptom attack you fear and avoid. If the attack you fear is not here, write it at the bottom of the list. We are not interested in sensations you simply dislike. Only check items you *fear*. (Note that a panic attack includes a number of feared sensations coming forcefully all at once.)

What are the symptom attacks that you fear?

- ☐ Panic attack or limited symptom attack

- ☐ Diarrhea or loss of bowel control

- ☐ Loss of bladder control

- ☐ Vomiting

- ☐ Fainting or passing out

- ☐ Falling

- ☐ Headache

- ☐ Other pain attacks: _____

- ☐ Asthma attack

- ☐ Other somatic ailments of a sporadic and unpredictable nature, such as attacks of epilepsy or colitis: _____

- ☐ Sudden surges of sorrow or sadness

- ☐ Sudden surges of anger

- ☐ Other: _____

_____

_____

_____

Fourth Component: The Feared Catastrophe

The final component of agoraphobia is the feared catastrophe, the outcome you fear could result from a symptom attack. It's your worst fear. It's the insanity or death or complete humiliation you fear will ultimately result from the attack. It is what you believe a symptom attack will lead to that causes the anxiety that you experience as an agoraphobic.

Compared to identifying the first three components, figuring out your feared catastrophe may be a more difficult task. Most agoraphobics encounter internal and external danger signals frequently and may have experienced a symptom attack numerous times. However, few if any agoraphobics have ever experienced the catastrophe they fear. Understandably, some of our clients have lost sight of the ultimate threat their symptom attack represents. They've convinced themselves, "I just don't like the feeling. That's why I hate those attacks." In other instances, they have a sense of the feared outcome but are confused because another part of them recognizes the irrationality of the fear. Again, in most cases, the feared catastrophe has not actually occurred. But let's qualify this a bit. If by "losing control" you mean crying or acting hysterically, doing so may *feel* like a catastrophe. Similarly, you might at one time or another have been ridiculed for having shown signs of anxiety (like trembling or blushing) and felt embarrassed but you weren't incapacitated. However, none of these events were catastrophic in an objective sense. Instead, you *perceive* yourself as unable to cope with these events.

The Four Types of Feared Catastrophe

All phobias can ultimately be reduced to four different types of feared catastrophes. The four basic categories are physical, psychological, social, and spiritual. Read about each below and think about which are most relevant to you. It is not unusual for someone to have more than one type of fear. Note that the fear of spiritual catastrophe, though sometimes found in other anxiety disorders, is seldom associated with agoraphobia. Most likely, your feared catastrophe falls into one of the first three categories. Check off the one/s that apply to you.

☐ Physical catastrophe: This category includes threats to the integrity of your body. It means death by various means (suffocation, heart attack, stroke, and so on), disabling injury, serious disease, and disfigurement.

☐ Psychological catastrophe: This means threats to the integrity of your mind or intellect. It includes going insane, losing control, losing intelligence, losing the ability to function, and experiencing permanent distress due to anxiety and inability to cope.

☐ Social catastrophe: This category has to do with threats to your social status. It includes severe rejection, criticism, disapproval, abandonment, humiliation, embarrassment, and shame. Fear of this catastrophe is often accompanied by the belief that you are incapable of coping with this kind of negative social experience.

☐ Spiritual catastrophe: These catastrophic fears include threats to your status with God or your spiritual well-being. They may include being judged or punished by God (going to hell) or suffering some other negative consequence related to your religious beliefs or spirituality.

Logical versus Felt Beliefs

If you are struggling to identify the underlying catastrophe, it may help you to know the difference between *logical* beliefs and *felt* beliefs. A logical belief is what you actually think (what you believe intellectually). A felt belief is what you feel (what your fear believes). Remember, logical beliefs and felt beliefs involve two different parts of the brain and are not always in agreement. If we were to ask you, "What's the worst thing you fear will happen if you experience a symptom attack?" you may answer, "Well I *know* nothing will happen!" This is your intellectual mind talking. It is your logical belief. Yet, if all of your mind believed there was nothing to fear, you would not feel anxious or avoid things. There would be no problem. Somewhere in your mind you are anticipating something bad happening.

So in response, let us rephrase the question this way, "What is your felt belief? What do you *fear* might happen?" The felt belief is illogical, but nonetheless it is the belief behind the fear you feel. As we mentioned in the introduction, fear-based irrational beliefs are not a sign you are unintelligent or cannot reason. Intelligent and well-educated people are as vulnerable to phobias as everyone else. As you try to discover the catastrophic outcome *you* fear, focus on what you feel will happen. Do not be distracted by your logical mind that may disrupt the process with thoughts like, "That's stupid!" or "I know better than to believe that!" or "That won't happen!" If part of you feels it, you are probably getting in touch with your feared catastrophe.

More Hints to Help You Identify Your Feared Catastrophe

Some people have coped with avoidance for so long they no longer ask themselves what the real fear is. If you are not immediately clear about the catastrophe you fear, there are several ways to help you clarify it. Select a circumstance you fear and ask yourself, "What exactly am I afraid will happen in this situation?" If this does not work, ask yourself, "What is the worst thing I fear will happen there?"

Sometimes a little exposure can help. Encounter something you fear, such as going to a mall, standing in line, or going for a walk outside, and then ask yourself, "What is the worst thing I fear will happen right now?" It is important to stay in the situation until you have the answer. If your answer is "I'm stuck," "I can't get out," "I'll run out," or even "I'll faint," pursue it further. These only describe a situation without saying why you fear it. Further questions are, "If I'm stuck here for a while, what's the most terrible thing that will happen? If I can't escape, what may happen? If I were to faint here, why would it be so bad?" (If you were to fall down, do you fear getting hurt or dying, or do you fear feeling embarrassed by people staring at you or trying to help you?) Remember to focus on what you *feel* will happen, not what you logically think. Try to stay with it until you find the answer.

A catastrophic fear can also be difficult to identify because it can evolve and change over time, sometimes changing from something more tangible to something more diffuse. Agoraphobia with fear of panic attacks, for instance, frequently involves fear of physical catastrophes like heart attack, stroke, or suffocation. After many events, the person realizes the feared catastrophe is not going to occur. Yet fears are resistant to extinction; they do not go away easily. The same situation continues to be associated with fear, and maybe other sensations become attached or conditioned to the fear. We said earlier that over time many agoraphobics fear losing control or being unable to cope, which they believe might lead to rejection by others or insanity. Note that these fears may be more elusive, harder to disprove. The emergency room does not provide you with definitive tests of your sanity or social acceptability.

If up to this point you still don't know the catastrophe you fear, take heart! We run into some clients who have this difficulty, and you are bravely doing the work on your own! We'll help you with an exercise, but first here's an example of how someone spontaneously realized what they feared. It came up in a group therapy session and illustrates some of the difficulties that arise. You may relate to them.

Unfolding the Feared Catastrophe: A Dialogue

Brian was participating in a group therapy session with seven other people. Here is the dialogue that took place.

Brian: I'm afraid, sitting in this room filled with people. *(External danger signal.)*

Therapist: What do you fear will happen?

Brian: My heart beats fast, my chest is tight, and I can't breathe well. *(Internal danger signal.)*

Therapist: And if you feel those sensations, what do you fear will happen?

Brian: I feel trapped and want to leave. *(He describes the situation and states the attempted solution or escape.)*

Therapist: Being in this room, everyone is confined for a while. Being trapped is more a description of the danger signal than the fear. You've said you feel this way also when stuck in traffic. Everyone in their car is then stuck, "trapped" if you will. Would you agree that not everyone stuck in traffic is afraid?

Brian: Yes.

Therapist: Then the question is still, what do you fear in this room with us while feeling rapid heartbeat, chest tightness, and difficulty breathing?

Brian: I fear I want to leave and if I did so, I'd feel embarrassed and then won't be able to come back next time.

Therapist: Fair enough, but let's try to go a bit deeper. Do you feel comfortable enough to proceed?

Brian: Yes.

Therapist: Note that wanting to leave is your attempted solution, an escape. *(She addresses the group.)* How do we know if something is an attempted solution?

Another group member: If I felt like Brian, I'd feel relief leaving!

Therapist: Right! Relief tells you that the behavior is an attempted solution. So, Brian, if you couldn't leave, what awful thing would happen here right now? What's the worst thing you feel could happen?

Brian: I'll have a panic attack and lose control, I guess.

Therapist: Now we are getting much closer. How would you lose control in a panic?

Brian: My mind will go blank and I won't be able to speak or make sense. *(Feared symptom attack.)*

Therapist: Okay, your feared symptom attack is maybe a panic attack with inability to speak or make sense. Is that so?

Brian: Oh, yes.

Therapist: And what would be so terrible if your mind went blank here and you would not speak or make sense?

Brian: I'll be totally embarrassed. I might not be able to come back to the group. I couldn't face them again. *(Feared catastrophe.)*

Therapist: We'll work on that fear. But for now we know the catastrophic outcome you fear: total embarrassment. And you alluded to the same fear when you said earlier that if you left, you wouldn't be able to return next time because you'd feel so embarrassed.

Brian's example is quite involved. Your exercise is much simpler. But if you get stuck, return to this example. You might be able to see how *you* get sidetracked. Then continue with your exercise.

Exercise: Unfolding Your Feared Catastrophe

1. Briefly describe an agoraphobic experience you've had that would make you very anxious if it happened today. Include both internal and external danger signals (such as, "I'm driving a car on a busy highway and all of a sudden I feel dizzy"). Select the elements of this scene by including the items from your lists of internal and external danger signals that appear earlier in this chapter. Write the scene here: _____

_____

_____

2. Referring to this scene, ask yourself, "And if this happened, why would *that* make me anxious? What am I afraid will happen next if I cannot escape and the sensations I fear continue to escalate?" Write the answer here: _____

   _____

   _____

3. Referring to your answer to the previous question, ask yourself, "And if that happened, why does that make me anxious? What am I afraid will happen next?" Write your answer here: _____

   _____

   _____

4. Referring to this last answer, ask yourself, "And if *that* happened, why does that make me anxious? What am I afraid will happen next?" Write your answer here: _____

   _____

   _____

Further instructions for this exercise: Continue this process until you have reached the ultimate catastrophe you feel could result from the symptom attack. It has to be something more than simply feeling bad. It should be something extreme, such as dying, or going insane, or being incapacitated with humiliation. Keep going until you reach an outcome that is truly severe. Do not censor your feelings with logical analysis. Remember, right now, what's important to identify is what you feel, not what you think. You need to know your worst fear. That is what drives your agoraphobia.

If you're trying to figure out whether you've gone far enough to unfold your feared catastrophe, whether you've taken it to its final conclusion, step back a moment. Look at the outcome you have written down and ask yourself, "Would other people be afraid if they thought this was going to happen to them?" If the answer is "yes," you're probably there.

4

Why Your Agoraphobia Has Not Gone Away

Where We're Going

We hope we've helped you gain a thorough understanding of agoraphobia, including the various components of your own fear. But there is one more aspect of agoraphobia you need to understand—what keeps this disabling problem going. In this chapter, you will learn why, despite logic and your best efforts to reason away your fears, agoraphobia persists. We will present a model that will illustrate how your agoraphobia is maintained. We'll give you examples first, and then you'll apply the model to yourself.

Most people who suffer from agoraphobia are discouraged when their fear does not subside, even when they tell themselves that their fear is unreasonable. They are understandably perplexed and frustrated. In some cases, they have encountered danger signals repeatedly. They may have experienced a symptom attack, or several, and have had numerous opportunities to discover the catastrophe they fear doesn't happen. They did not die. They did not lose their sanity. No real catastrophe resulted from the symptom attack. And yet, their fear persists. Why have they not learned there is nothing to fear? The answer lies in understanding the counterproductive effects of avoidant coping.

Counterproductive Effects of Avoidance

> Fred lived in a peaceful suburban town called Smithville. Every day, he would sit in a lawn chair in his backyard dutifully holding an elephant gun. One day his neighbor, Steve, noticed what Fred was doing and yelled over the fence, "Hey, Fred! What in the heck are you doing with that elephant gun? Fred replied, "I'm keeping the elephants away." Steve couldn't believe what he was hearing. Fred did not appear to be joking, so Steve couldn't resist stating the obvious. "But Fred," he said, "There are no elephants in Smithville. "Fred smiled and said, "See how well it works?"

Fred's use of the elephant gun is not unlike the ways in which agoraphobia sufferers cope with their fear. Fred has a fear that elephants will stampede his home, despite the fact no elephant has ever been sighted in Smithville. Fred's use of the gun prevents him from learning that there are no elephants because he attributes the lack of elephants to the presence of the gun, rather than concluding that there are no elephants at all. Although the gun makes him feel safer in the moment, the long-term effects of the gun are highly detrimental. The gun allows Fred to maintain the fundamentally flawed belief that elephants do exist in Smithville. As long as Fred uses the gun, his elephant phobia will not go away.

Fred's use of the gun is a form of avoidant coping. *Avoidant coping* is any behavior or tactic a person uses to avert danger. When a person's perception of danger is accurate, avoidant coping is useful. It is useful, for example, to avoid sticking your hand into a hot flame. However, when your assessment of danger is not accurate, as is the case with agoraphobia or any other anxiety disorder, avoidant coping can be harmful. Avoidant coping interferes with learning. It prevents people from discovering that they are wrong about the threats they perceive. We will explain more about how avoidant coping maintains agoraphobia, but first it is helpful to understand the different types of avoidant coping.

Staying Away from Danger Altogether

The most obvious form of avoidant coping is called *primary avoidance*, or "Don't go there!" Primary avoidance is when you stay away from a danger signal completely; for example, when a person with a fear of heights refuses to go anywhere higher than the second floor of a building. Primary avoidance is the most complete form of avoidance. It is also the most harmful because an irrational fear never has the opportunity to be contradicted by reality. Most people recognize that avoidance interferes with the quality of their lives but do not realize that it has an even worse side effect: the perpetuation of their fear. *Not only does the phobia not go away, but fear grows in the absence of the feared situation.* In the mind, the notion that a situation is dangerous gets repeated over and over. Primary avoidance is not the only way to perpetuate a fear, however. There are many other, more subtle forms of avoidance that are also harmful. Read on.

Trying to Make It Safer When You Can't Get Away

Primary avoidance cannot always be achieved. It is often not practical, for one thing. For example, agoraphobics may be afraid to go to work, but they need the money. Furthermore, internal danger signals are typically not controllable, which makes it very difficult to avoid experiencing them. How do you completely avoid light-headed feelings or nausea? When primary avoidance is not feasible, human beings develop *secondary avoidance* strategies. These are the strategies you use to make the situation safer when danger signals cannot be avoided altogether. Using *safety signals* and engaging in *safety behaviors* are two forms of secondary avoidance.

Safety Signals

Safety signals refer to the objects or people you use to feel safer in the presence of danger signals. They help create the perception that the danger is either less likely or less severe than it would otherwise be. Examples of safety signals are tranquilizers, cell phones, and water. Many people without agoraphobia carry these things with them, but these items have a different meaning in the context of agoraphobia. Let us check this out with you. If you like to carry water or a cell phone with you, but you could be without them, then they do not constitute safety signals. They are safety signals only if you must have such devices because they help you cope with your anxiety. The most powerful safety signal for many agoraphobics, and maybe for you, is the presence of another person. You perceive this "safe" person as a rescuer who could save you in case symptom attacks become overwhelming. Remember, if you can do everything, but only with another person along, you still have agoraphobia. Listed below are some common safety signals used by people with agoraphobia. Check off the ones you use.

What are your safety signals?

☐ Presence of a safe person

☐ Medications (like tranquilizers), even if you hardly ever take them, including an empty pill bottle that represents the medication

☐ Cell phone

☐ Telephone numbers of nearby hospitals

☐ Small brown paper bag (to breathe into in case of hyperventilation)

☐ Water, sodas or food

☐ Lucky charms or other superstitious items

☐ Alcohol

☐ Other (any object that is supposed to save you from feeling too anxious or prevent the feared consequence from happening): _____

_____

_____

_____

Safety Behaviors

Safety behaviors are actions you take in the presence of danger signals to "save" yourself from the symptom attack or its dreaded consequences. Safety behaviors can be very subtle. You may not realize you're doing them or why you're doing them. You may have convinced yourself you're acting this way for some other, practical reason. Take, for example, always sitting in the back of a cinema by the aisle in order to make a quick exit, or sitting down whenever you feel anxiety sensations because you think you might otherwise faint. You may think you do these things for convenience or comfort, but think again. Do these behaviors make you feel safer? If so, they are probably a form of avoidance and, remember, avoidance is not adaptive in the long run.

Below are common behaviors that agoraphobia sufferers engage in to feel safe in the presence of danger signals. Check off each one that pertains to you. These are just a few examples. Feel free to write in others.

Which of the following safety behaviors do you use?

☐ Distracting yourself (behavioral or mental avoidance, such as driving with the radio on, focusing your attention on something else, reading, listening to music)

☐ Focusing on escape plans (looking for exit signs in department stores), sitting or standing near exits

☐ Grasping the steering wheel tightly

☐ Driving only in the slow lane for a quick exit, if necessary

☐ Leaning on walls, furniture, shopping carts (to prevent fainting, falling from weak legs)

☐ Sitting down so as not to faint

☐ Asking or looking for nearby bathrooms, even if you do not need to use the bathroom right then

☐ Trying to relax (to control the symptom attack)

☐ Initiating conversations with others (so as not to pay attention to sensations)

☐ Asking others for reassurance

☐ Pushing through the situation (to get out quickly)

☐ Watching or restricting what you eat or drink

☐ Wearing sunglasses, loose clothing, or anything else to prevent the feared attack

☐ Doing things on "good" versus "bad" days

☐ Other (any behavior or action that is supposed to save you from feeling too anxious or prevent the feared consequence from happening): _____

_____

_____

_____

How Catastrophic Thinking and Avoidance Fuel Agoraphobia

The cognitive behavioral model for the treatment of anxiety disorders does not try to explain why a person first begins to misjudge danger. Instead, it explains why those misjudgments continue and how to change them. Humans tend to overpredict danger, to err on the side of caution. Better safe than sorry is our brain's motto. However, we also have a system for correcting errors. When we misjudge threat, we can eventually correct it. But in the case of agoraphobia (as well as other anxiety disorders), your misjudgments do not get corrected. You continue seeing a situation as dangerous, even if there is no true evidence of danger.

Does that mean if you have agoraphobia you are stubborn? Not at all. It means your emotional brain has not received the information it needs to correct your perception of danger. And it is avoidant coping that prevents it from getting that information.

Now let's look at how avoidant coping fits into the cycle that perpetuates agoraphobia. People with agoraphobia exaggerate (overpredict) how likely and how serious danger is. They misinterpret neutral situations as dangerous and become anxious. They then cope with the anxiety by resorting to avoidant coping. The avoidance prevents them from correcting their false assumptions. If you are agoraphobic, this means you will respond exactly the same way the next time you encounter the situation. And the cycle continues.

It may help to understand this cycle by considering a few examples. First, we will use the example of an insect phobia, since this basic cycle occurs in all phobias. Then we will look at two examples of agoraphobia.

Jack's Story

Jack has an insect phobia. The danger signals for his phobia include any sights or sounds he associates with bugs. The feared catastrophe is that he will be stung or bitten by an insect, become seriously ill, and die. A fly buzzing around the back patio is a danger signal to Jack. He misinterprets the situation as a signal that he is in danger. He believes his catastrophic fear (death) will happen. He becomes anxious and responds by running inside (primary avoidance) or by staying outside and spraying insect repellent on himself and around the patio (secondary avoidance). Because he engages in avoidant coping, Jack continues to believe insects are dangerous. "After all," he tells himself, "I would have been bitten and died if I had stayed on the patio without the repellent." Now, despite having no actual evidence that insects are dangerous, his mistaken belief about the danger of insects is strengthened. The next time Jack is outside and sees a fly buzzing around, he will make the same misappraisal of threat and respond in the same maladaptive way.

Now let's look at two cases of agoraphobia that follow the same basic model. Then see if you can apply the pattern to yourself. Fill out worksheet 1 after you've read the following examples. It will illustrate in black-and-white how your agoraphobia is maintained and will help you understand the work that lies ahead.

The Model	**Paul's Case**
Danger signals (What internal sensations in what external situation?) ↓	Feels light-headed while riding the subway ↓
→*Misinterpretation of the danger signal* ↓	"I won't be able to get out. I will faint, make a total fool of myself, and be unable to cope." ↓
Emotional response ↓	Anxiety ↓
Avoidant coping ↓	a) Does not avoid the subway because it is his only way to get to work; he never uses it otherwise. b) If the subway stops for a while, he gets off at the next stop and takes a bus or a cab. c) Takes the subway early enough to get a seat. Carries a cell phone. If too anxious, he calls his wife. Though he cannot say what bothers him, she knows and gives him reassurance. Sometimes stops at the bar after work to have a drink before taking the subway home. ↓
└*Absence of a corrective experience* (No new learning takes place on an emotional level.)	Paul never learns that he will not faint from a panic. Also, if for some medical reason he ever were to faint, he does not realize that people would likely help, not put him down for it.

Paul's avoidance prevents him from having the experience he needs in order to be convinced the feared catastrophe will not happen. Therefore, he continues to believe the feared catastrophe will occur, which means he'll again become anxious the next time he has light-headed feelings while riding the subway.

Note that in Paul's case, his fear is not incapacitation from fainting but rather the resulting embarrassment. His fear of subways and buses has not subsided because he uses them only when he has to, he escapes if he can when he starts to feel light-headed, he takes the train early enough to be able to sit (to decrease the chances of fainting), he carries a cell phone, and after work he sometimes has a drink before facing the subway again. All of these avoidance behaviors prevent him from finding out that nothing catastrophic will happen.

In Susie's case, described below, the catastrophic fear is not the sense of inability to cope with the migraine, but going insane as a result. In her example, she could not limit her outings to exactly fifteen minutes from home, but she tried. She resorted to avoiding going out for more than fifteen minutes at a time, escaping (returning home) as soon as she thought that she might get a migraine, scanning for the way her head felt, seeking reassurance about her mental stability, and doing most activities with her husband.

The Model	**Susie's Example**
Danger signals (What internal sensations in what external situation?)	A migraine aura more than fifteen minutes from home
↓	↓
Misinterpretation of the danger signal	"I will get a migraine, not be able to cope with it, and go insane."
↓	↓
Emotional response	Anxiety
↓	↓
Avoidant coping	a) Tries not to travel alone more than fifteen minutes from home. b) Escapes as soon as she feels the aura coming on. c) Scans for tension in her head. Seeks reassurance about her mental stability. Does most activities with her husband.
↓	↓
Absence of a corrective experience (No new learning takes place on an emotional level)	Susie never learns that she can cope with a migraine while alone outside without going insane.

Just like Paul and Jack, Susie engages in avoidance, which keeps her from having the opportunity to learn she can handle a migraine headache on her own and will not go insane. Without the corrective experience she needs,

Susie's beliefs about the danger of migraines go unchanged and she is destined to be afraid in the future whenever she experiences migraine auras away from home.

Now it is your turn to use worksheet 1 to see how catastrophic thinking and avoidant coping fuel your phobia. The purpose of this worksheet is to illustrate how your agoraphobia is maintained. That means we want you to pick only one set of danger signals (one type of sensation in one particular situation), and proceed through the worksheet. Review the previous examples, if necessary, for guidance.

Worksheet 1: How Catastrophic Thinking and Avoidant Coping Fuel Your Phobia

Danger signals
(What internal sensations
in what external situation?)

↓

1) Describe one combination of danger signals (at least one internal and one external) that makes you anxious: _____

_____

_____

↓

→*Misinterpretation of the danger signal*

↓

2) Why is that combination of danger signals dangerous? What symptom attack and catastrophe might it lead to? _____

_____

_____

↓

Emotional response
(anxiety, panic)

↓

3) What emotion do you experience when in the presence of this combination of danger signals? _____

_____

↓

Avoidant coping

↓

4) List the ways in which you try to avoid the symptom attack and the feared catastrophe: _____

_____

_____

_____

_____

↓

Absence of a corrective experience
(No new learning takes place on an emotional level.)

5) How has your avoidance interfered with learning? (What do you still need to learn in order to feel different about the danger signals?) _____

_____

Before reading further, take a moment to review some main points we've covered in this chapter:

- Phobic reactions are based on misinterpretations of danger.

- Avoiding danger signals prolongs the phobia because you never learn what really happens and continue to believe there is danger.

- Avoidance may help you feel better temporarily and may get you through a situation, but it will not help you get better in the long run.

- Exposure to danger signals in the absence of any avoidance is the best remedy for a phobia.

5

How to Make Your Agoraphobia Go Away

Where We're Going

In the previous chapter, you learned why your agoraphobia has not gone away. Now we'll tell you about research findings that indicate how agoraphobia can be reversed. That's the good news. It can be reversed. This chapter will give you the basis for the steps you'll be taking in your road to recovery. We also provide you with some information about medications that could assist your efforts.

There are many problems for which effective help is not available. Fortunately, agoraphobia is not among them. Agoraphobia sufferers have reason to be optimistic. A great deal has been learned about how to overcome this troubling disorder.

Overcoming Agoraphobia: What the Research Says

The cornerstone of phobia treatment is exposure to what is feared. In vivo exposure is the most effective form of treatment for agoraphobia. *In vivo exposure* means confronting something in real life (as opposed to confronting it in your imagination). In agoraphobia, in vivo exposure involves exposing yourself to external danger signals.

Another form of exposure is also helpful. It is called *interoceptive exposure* and involves exposing yourself to internal danger signals. That is, you purposefully experience and learn to respond differently to the internal sensations that trigger your anxiety. These two forms of exposure, in vivo and introceptive, are an integral part of the program in this book.

The therapeutic effects of exposure have been demonstrated in numerous scientific studies on the treatment of phobias. The majority of people who receive this treatment get better. Because exposure is such an important part of our program, we want you to understand it well. First we will review how exposure works, then we'll discuss the elements of successful exposure. We will also briefly describe other things you'll need to learn and do to recover from agoraphobia.

How Exposure Works

How does exposure help you with your agoraphobia? We have purposefully posed this as a question because there is no definitive answer. There are several different theories. Here is a summary of the theories, as so aptly reviewed by Barlow (1988). None of these theories explains the process fully. The learning that takes place during exposure may be too complex to be fully captured by a single theory.

1. The *habituation theory* proposes that when repeatedly exposed to a fearful situation, you become desensitized to these danger signals and your reactions gradually weaken, especially your physiological responses.

2. According to the *extinction theory,* you acquire new learning when you repeatedly encounter a feared signal and the dreaded consequence does not occur.

3. A biologically-based theory, the *toughening-up theory,* is based on research showing that repeated exposure produces biochemical changes, leading then to more behavioral changes. Of interest here is that animal and subsequent clinical studies have shown that drugs that reduce anxious arousal may interfere with toughening-up, suggesting that such medications could interfere with the full benefits of exposure.

4. The *self-efficacy theory* states that exposure works through an increased sense of mastery over the situation you fear. When you feel a sense of mastery over a situation, you are more likely to enter it, even if you are afraid.

5. The more comprehensive *emotional processing theory* elaborates on how learning occurs during exposure. When you are engaged in one prolonged exposure trial (one to two hours), you learn through short-term habituation that anxiety does not last forever; it diminishes during the exposure. With repeated exposure trials, you learn that the feared catastrophe does not occur. In addition, you learn that the experience (of anxiety) itself is not so bad. If your exposure is incomplete (because of the use of safety devices), your emotional processing will be incomplete. Does this sound familiar? Safety devices interfere with full learning. (The technical explanation is that distraction of any kind prevents full attention on and therefore inadequate processing of your fear.)

6. The *cognitive theory* suggests that exposure provides the information you need to change your beliefs about the danger of a situation. The exposure is seen as a behavioral experiment people can use to test their faulty beliefs. When their expectations about danger do not happen, they adjust their beliefs.

These different theories are not necessarily incompatible. The processes they describe may work together. What these theories all recognize is the human capacity to learn and to change through experience. And it is a particular type of learning that seems to be necessary for change to occur.

The Importance of Experiential Learning

We said before that simple logic and reasoning do not usually work by themselves to overcome phobias. This is because felt beliefs operate in the experiential mind, as opposed to the rational mind. To understand this idea better, consider another type of felt belief: prejudice. Like agoraphobic beliefs, prejudice is based on partial information. It involves misinterpretation (overgeneralization) of information and is maintained by avoidance. Most of us have some prejudice, even if we do not like to think so. Assume for a moment you had a prejudice against bald men. Let's say you felt all bald men were mean. How would you go about changing that prejudice? Gathering facts about bald men, perhaps. Maybe you'd challenge the logic of the theory that bald men are mean. Whatever else you might do, the most powerful way to change how you feel about bald men would be to spend some time with them. You would then discover, through experiential learning, that bald men are tall or short, young or old, intelligent or not very bright, nice or mean—in other words, no different from anyone else. Your actual experiences would contradict your original felt belief. Over time, your belief would change (if you did not engage in avoidance). You would start to look at bald men as simply people.

This example demonstrates the importance of *experiential learning*. The emotional brain does not change with logic alone. New experiences work because they affect how you feel about something; they have a direct impact on the emotional brain. To recover from agoraphobia, you must face the situations you fear, eventually without any of your avoidant coping strategies. You may use distraction or other strategies to get through an exposure, and you may succeed at getting through the situation. But, remember, coping this way will not help you get better. If the thought of getting rid of all your avoidant strategies makes you anxious, it's understandable. Keep in mind, you'll be going at your own pace, taking things a step at a time.

Essential Elements to Facilitate Change

Barlow (1988) points to four elements that must be present in order for change to occur in fear. These are listed and elaborated upon below.

There must be a change in action. The exaggerated vigilance we described earlier in the book is related to the readiness to take action; the agoraphobic consciously or subconsciously looks for danger signals, ultimately to escape. Exposure is the opposite action. As you approach and stay fully in the situation, your change in action brings about a new way of feeling. This is a key part of what you will soon be doing.

Another crucial element is gaining control. The key is to learn to *feel* in control, even if the symptom attacks occur and seem unpredictable and uncontrollable. People with agoraphobia do not feel in control because they look for every way in which they are trapped instead of, like average people, every way in which they are *not* trapped. Even in a truly confining situation like an airplane, you can be totally free, not trapped, in your mind. In other words, perceiving that you have control is crucial. That means knowing what you can and cannot control. We will help you focus on the things you can control and let go of things you cannot control.

Cognitive (mental) work seems to be beneficial, primarily in helping protect against relapse. In this vein, you will learn how to directly challenge your negative automatic thoughts.

The use of truly helpful coping strategies increases your sense of control and can help you to achieve mastery. Great care must be taken, however, that these strategies do not end up being used as safety devices that interfere with learning. We will help you distinguish between helpful and nonhelpful strategies.

The Most Effective Ways to Do Exposure

Exposure has been done in many ways, some more successful than others. As you already know, safety devices need to be eliminated eventually. Below is information on effective ways to do exposure, based on research findings.

You can do graduated or graded exposure; both work well. Bigger tasks are broken into smaller steps, starting with the easier ones. This makes exposure manageable, and most people opt for this approach. Another approach, *flooding,* is when you start with a more advanced, difficult task and stay with it until your anxiety comes down. Flooding works (Hahlweg et al. 2001), but most people don't want to experience high levels of anxiety for a longer period of time, which often occurs with flooding. We do not advise flooding in situations where you may have diarrhea or a migraine attack, especially if they actually occur. In these instances, a gradual approach is recommended.

Try to expose yourself for a prolonged period of time until your anxiety and urge to escape have subsided (Drummond 1993). The time varies, but it can take up to one to two hours. When the time of each encounter is usually brief (using elevators and escalators or driving over a bridge), the situation can be prolonged by repeating the exposure multiple times in a row (Zuercher-White 1997). We call it *repeated exposure loops.* As you do these exposures, you can move to the next more difficult step before fully mastering the previous step. Your progress will be faster than if you keep doing the same exposure until you are perfectly comfortable with it. Even so, be sure and pace yourself so you don't take on too much too quickly and wind up putting off the exposure work that you need to do to recover.

Do exposures as often as possible. The more time spent on exposures, the better. Six to seven hours a week or more (Fava et al. 1997), spread over three or four days, is desirable. Daily exposure sessions are even more effective. Of course, you need to do what is realistic for your situation. Just remember, the less exposure you do each week, the longer your recovery will take.

Do exposures alone; a coach can help you if needed. There are definite advantages to doing exposures alone. If you use a coach, you are dependent on the other person's willingness and availability, as well as his or her schedule. Your coach may not be supportive in the right way, or you may fear disappointing your coach. However, sometimes a coach is helpful, particularly during certain challenging stages of your recovery (like crossing a bridge for the first time). If you do use a coach, do so only once or twice. Do the exposure alone *as soon as possible.* Handling a less difficult situation by yourself can be a more meaningful accomplishment than completing a highly difficult task with someone helping you. And eventually, you will want to be able to do things on your own anyway.

Expose yourself to *all* avoided situations. Omitting some avoided situations usually indicates continued catastrophic thinking and may increase your risk of relapse (Barlow and Craske 1994). The more situations you leave unchallenged, the greater the chances of relapse.

Expose yourself to feared internal sensations (interoceptive exposure). Interoceptive exposure has also been shown to enhance treatment in panic disorder with agoraphobia. To repeatedly bring on feared bodily sensations (yes, on purpose) helps a person learn to deal with unexpected and undesirable symptoms. Exposure to the most feared sensations more fully tests the belief that a catastrophic outcome will result. Participants in one study reported less fear of panic sensations and had fewer panic attacks when they had used this procedure (Craske et al. 1997).

The Role of Medication

One thing many people with agoraphobia ask is whether or not they should take medication. This is a natural question, given the discomfort and numerous symptoms that often accompany agoraphobia. The answer is, "It depends." You didn't think the answer would be simple, did you?

There is a wide variety of attitudes and opinions about the role of medication for people with agoraphobia. Many physicians and therapists strongly recommend medication. Others advise against it. Some patients insist on taking medication. Others won't even consider it, either for philosophical reasons or because they are afraid the drug will create unpleasant side effects or make them feel less in control. So what's the right approach for you?

Research suggests that drug treatments can help reduce the symptoms of agoraphobia, particularly in the short run. However, research and our clinical experience also suggest that there are some limitations and disadvantages to using medication with this disorder. Although most medications used for agoraphobia are not acutely dangerous, as some patients fear, they can have unpleasant side effects. You may also want to consider the extra expense and possible lifestyle adjustments that come with medication. However, the biggest disadvantage of medication is that in some cases it can interfere with your recovery, because it can interfere with the learning that needs to take place. If agoraphobia sufferers start to believe that the drug they are taking prevents the catastrophe they fear, then taking medicine becomes another form of avoidant coping that can limit recovery in the long run. Studies have shown that agoraphobia patients who take medication have a higher relapse rate (particularly when the drug is discontinued) than those who receive cognitive behavioral therapy.

You may find some of this puzzling if you have been told your condition is due to a chemical imbalance in the brain, a position promoted by pharmaceutical companies and some health-care professionals. Almost certainly, biochemical irregularities are involved in agoraphobia—and every other anxiety disorder, for that matter. But reducing the disorder to a chemical imbalance is simplistic and misleading. It ignores the mutual influence of brain and behavior. It also implies that brain activity can only be influenced by chemical intervention. The truth is that your brain and your behavior work together and constantly influence each other. Behavioral exposure actually produces biochemical changes, which in turn facilitate the learning process. Medication and cognitive behavioral therapy both influence brain chemistry. Yet the learning that results from cognitive behavioral therapy usually produces more lasting effects. There are good reasons to consider taking medication for agoraphobia, but having a "chemical imbalance" is not one of them.

So what are some good reasons to take medication for agoraphobia? Some people experience such disturbing levels of anxiety that they feel unable to function without medication. Some try to do the work without medication first and then encounter difficulties that can be helped by medication. Others may have severe depression or other problems, in addition to their phobia, for which a drug treatment may be helpful. If any of these scenarios applies to your situation, medication might help you feel good enough to attempt the recovery work you might otherwise never try.

If medication is something you are contemplating or have already been prescribed, here are two guidelines to consider:

1. If you are on medication, wait until you are on a steady dose, then follow this program. It is usually better not to begin exposure work at the same time you're switching or adjusting medication.

2. Once you've made a sufficient amount of progress with this work, you may be able to taper off medication. Usually this is done slowly, over time. You can discuss this with your psychiatrist or other prescribing provider.

If you are still in the early stages of selecting or adjusting to medication, you may want to wait until your medication regimen has been established before you move forward with this program. If you have decided to try this program without medication, or if you have already adjusted to the medication you are taking, please proceed to the next chapter.

Commonly Prescribed Medications for Agoraphobia

When medication is used for agoraphobia, antidepressants are usually recommended, in particular SSRIs (selective serotonin reuptake inhibitors). The SSRIs include Prozac, Paxil, Zoloft, Celexa, Luvox, and Lexapro. These drugs tend to have fewer side effects than some of the other antidepressants. If you are considering taking drugs, however, your physician can help you select the right medication for you.

It is better if you can get by without using benzodiazepines (Valium, Xanax, Ativan) or other tranquilizers, which can create dependency problems and, at high doses, can interfere with learning. Sometimes these drugs are used temporarily to assist people while they're waiting for an antidepressant to take effect. When a tranquilizer needs to be used, it is better to take it on a regular schedule than on an as-needed basis and to avoid taking a very high dose. Taking a drug on a regular schedule at a moderate dose reduces the chances that you'll rely on medicine to cope with acute anxiety and makes the drug less likely to interfere with learning.

6

Some Final Things to Consider Before You Start

Where We're Going

Now you're almost ready to tackle your agoraphobia, but not quite. There are a few more things to consider before you begin. In this chapter, we'll alert you to some common pitfalls and discuss ways to approach the recovery process that will enhance your chances for success.

Now is the time to ask, "Is this important to me? Does this problem have a serious enough impact on my life for me to devote the time and effort necessary to change it?" If so, read further. You certainly want to know the best way to approach your recovery. We want you to succeed and avoid some of the common pitfalls.

Common Pitfalls

Over the years, we have observed several common pitfalls that hamper recovery from agoraphobia. If you find yourself doing any of these things, think again. You could be jeopardizing your recovery.

Not scheduling the time to do the work, or trying to squeeze it in. Doing exposures for fifteen minutes on Sunday morning won't do it. Trying to squeeze in the time somewhere does not produce success. You already know that overcoming agoraphobia is difficult work; it does not happen by itself. If you try to add exposure work to everything else in your life, you'll feel overwhelmed, tired, and irritable. Therefore, you must be willing to give up something else in your life for awhile and make the time you need to do this right. It may mean not attending your son's ball games, not doing your volunteer job, or paying someone else to clean your house. Something has to give. Otherwise your exposures will suffer.

Waiting for a good day. You may be tempted to put your exposures off until you have a good day, when you are feeling less anxious. People with agoraphobia monitor how they feel each day and act accordingly. This may very well be the case with you. On good days, you feel like you can conquer a great deal. On bad days, you feel vulnerable. A bad day is usually determined by stressful events or worries, including worrying about having a feared symptom attack. If you wait for good days, however, your progress will be much slower.

Reading this book without doing the exercises. Intellectual insight and good intentions will not produce change. You must apply the principles you learn to your everyday life.

Doing the work only if you're assured of not feeling too anxious. This is like waiting for a good day. It means you are willing to do the work as long as you do not have symptoms. While we know that they are highly unpleasant, symptom attacks will always be a possibility. If you carefully try to do everything so that you won't get too anxious you will not become free of your fears.

Depending too much on a coach or companion. You may want someone else to do exposures with you to create the illusions that nothing bad can happen, or that the coach will rescue you if it does. Relying on others will never set you free. The confidence must come from within you.

Giving up because you've tried before. You might actually have consulted a psychotherapist or psychiatrist for help, but without success. Traditional psychotherapy, relaxation techniques, and medications do not usually make phobias go away. There is no need to be discouraged. You may not have had the right help. Even if you had proper phobia therapy (cognitive behavioral therapy), there may be a good reason why it didn't work. Were you ready and committed to do the work? Did you participate fully? If not, perhaps you're ready now.

Quitting because you don't feel ready. We hope you'll decide to do this work. But if you decide you're not ready, continue reading until the end of this chapter. If you still don't feel ready, take a break. However, keep this book in a visible place, on your dresser or desk, so that you won't forget it. Hopefully, you'll be ready soon.

Sabotaging yourself. This is when you do things that will obviously jeopardize your recovery efforts, like taking on a stressful new job right when you're beginning to work on your agoraphobia. You may do this for many reasons. Look deep within yourself. Are you making yourself pay for something you feel guilty about? Is the disability of your agoraphobia preventing you from having to deal with something else that is difficult in your life (like a bad marriage or a career change)? If so, you may want to seek professional help.

Putting yourself down. This is common in people with agoraphobia. They belittle themselves for having the problem or for not having recovered sufficiently. Do you do this to yourself? If this is the case, your task will be that much harder. The road to recovery is not smooth. Your progress will be a lot harder if you put yourself down at every bump in the road.

Letting depression stop you. If you suffer from a level of depression that prevents you from focusing on this task and doing the work, you should probably treat the depression first. You are likely to need professional help. However, if your depression is not too severe and is secondary to your agoraphobia, you should be okay. The depression should lift as your agoraphobia improves.

Requirements for Successful Recovery

Here are some things you can do that will facilitate your recovery. These are the things we have observed our more successful clients do. You may have already guessed some of them. Taking these steps will give you the best chance to overcome your agoraphobia.

Be sure you have the necessary motivation. This is the very first requirement. Ultimately, all else follows from this. What does necessary motivation mean? It means you make recovery a priority, giving it your energy and time. It also means the willingness to experience discomfort—sometimes even high anxiety.

Devote a sufficient amount of time to this program. You need time to read this book, fill out the worksheets, and do the exposures to internal sensations. In addition, the amount of time devoted to in vivo exposures is crucial. Six to seven hours a week (unless your agoraphobia is exceedingly mild), spread over a minimum of three to four days, is usually needed. If you do exposures five to seven days a week, your progress will be faster. Remember that the amount of time spent on exposures equals the degree of improvement. When people spend less time, they usually progress more slowly. The more restricted you are (if you fear walking outside or driving alone anywhere), the more time you will need for exposures. If you are totally housebound, you will probably need professional help and maybe a coach to assist you.

Plan your exposures in advance. Exposures do not come naturally. You need to plan them, setting what days and what times. For most people, the best way to do this is to plan ahead, such as on the weekend for the upcoming week. *For the vast majority of people, this is the only way exposures will be completed on a consistent basis.* We recommend it. Put exposures in your schedule, so you don't need to debate on a daily basis whether or when to do them. Scheduling ahead also gets you around the good-versus-bad-day problem. In fact, the most important learning occurs on bad days. When the exposures are scheduled, you'll hit good, bad, and neutral days. You'll learn to do things under different circumstances. To make an analogy, most people don't go to work only on days they feel great. Everyone goes to work at times not feeling well physically or emotionally. You do your best.

Take advantage of unplanned opportunities for exposure. Spontaneous exposures are the unplanned encounters with danger signals that occur as part of everyday life. It is therapeutic to take advantage of these incidental exposures. For instance, if restaurants make you anxious and a coworker asks you out to lunch, try to accept the invitation. Take it as a challenge; you can gain from it.

Coping with these situations in a nonavoidant way is part of the recovery process. However, spontaneous exposures are no substitute for planned exposures. Planned exposures are the exercises you set out to do ahead of time. They move you steadily forward. They are the exposures that you initiate and control. Your main progress comes from them. Spontaneous exposures help reinforce and generalize what you gain from planned exposures. You need both to succeed.

Recognize and use your strengths. Agoraphobia does not encompass all of you. You have strengths that you can tap. Are you patient and kind, a good person to talk to? Do you use good judgment? Do you learn well? Are you a good observer? See how you can apply your strengths to phobic situations.

Reward yourself. Many people don't appreciate what they accomplish. For example, after going to the store alone for ten minutes for the first time in ten years, one client reflected, "That's nothing. Everyone can do that!" Instead, we recommend that you tell yourself what a great step you took. Whenever you do something that you were unable to do before, you need to recognize it for the accomplishment it is. Even if you do not finish an exposure as planned, give yourself credit for what you did accomplish. If you did more than you used to do, you were successful. Don't hesitate to give yourself concrete rewards as well. For bigger steps, buy yourself flowers, go to a movie, phone a friend long-distance. You earned it.

Prepare ahead of time for your exposures. Ask yourself, "How can I best prepare myself for this exposure so that I will maximize my sense of mastery?" Ask yourself further, "What is fearful to me about this upcoming step and how can I cope with it?" Rehearse the difficulties you expect and plan on how to handle them. We will teach you coping strategies that you may find helpful.

Take some time afterward to review your exposures. It is also important to make sure you take time to review what you've learned from each exposure. After each exposure, take a few minutes to recall what actually occurred and to answer a few questions: What did your fear predict would happen? What did you predict would happen based on your work in this book? Which prediction represents a more accurate account of what occurred?

A Quick Review of Key Points

Sometime during the process of working on their problem, many of our clients temporarily forget or get confused about some of the key principles of treatment. Anxiety has a way of steering people off course. You may find yourself in a similar position at some point. This is perfectly understandable. Much of what we've been telling you is new information, and some of it may be completely incompatible with what you have thought or been told in the past. Beware! Fear can trick you. It can confuse you and tempt you to return to old ways of thinking, right at the very time you need clarity the most.

You're getting ready to deal with the things you've been avoiding. Your anticipatory anxiety may be up a little. Your fear may be telling you not to listen to the things we are saying. It may be trying to confuse you. Don't let it succeed. Now is a good time to clarify your thinking. Let's review some key principles.

Don't forget these key points. If you have agoraphobia, remember:

- You fear experiencing a symptom attack in certain situations.

- You fear this attack because you believe it will result in some catastrophe.

- Your perception of this danger is inaccurate.

- Your misperception of danger has been maintained by your avoidance.

- Your misperception of danger must change for you to overcome your phobia.

- Your misperception of danger cannot be changed by logical persuasion alone.

- Your misperception of danger can be changed by corrective experiences, or exposure.

- The corrective experiences you need must convince your emotional brain that symptom attacks do not lead to catastrophe.

- Changing your misperception of danger means gaining the emotional confidence that you'll be able to deal with whatever happens.

Keep these points in mind as you progress to part 2 of this book and through the remaining steps of your recovery, and you won't lose sight of what you're doing. Return to this section of the book at any time you feel confused or when you feel tempted to fall back on old (avoidant) ideas or strategies. Part 2 represents the culmination of everything you've learned so far. So let's get going!

PART 2

What You Need to Do

In part 2, we'll teach you the concrete steps you'll need to follow for your recovery. They consist of setting goals, learning to use helpful coping strategies, and developing a new perspective about your fear. And, most importantly, you'll learn to challenge your beliefs about your feared catastrophe more directly by exposing yourself to internal and external danger signals.

7

Step 1. Setting Recovery Goals and Objectives

Where We're Going

Before embarking on a journey, it's always helpful to know where you're headed. In this chapter, you will learn why it's important to set goals and objectives. They define your path and ultimate success. And we will teach you how to develop the goals and objectives that will define your victory over agoraphobia.

The exposure work that lies ahead is difficult because you'll be confronting your fears directly. It's easy to get discouraged. At times, you may be tempted to settle for the restricted lifestyle imposed by your agoraphobia and forget why you're going through all this effort. This is why goals and objectives are so important and why they need to be crystal clear. You want to know, from the outset, where you're heading, what gains you want to make, and what you want to get out of this.

Developing Goals and Objectives

If you're still not sure why goals are important, think of the analogy of taking a class. The goal of a class is for you to learn something, such as English literature or calculus. Every time you attend a class or do your homework, you are engaging in tasks that will lead you to your goal. Having a goal helps, especially if you find learning new things particularly tedious or difficult. Remembering the reason you're pursuing an education helps you through the tough times in class and keeps you focused.

A goal is a statement summarizing what you want to accomplish. In this case, your goal should reflect what you want to accomplish by overcoming agoraphobia. Goals are the reasons you're trying to recover.

An objective is a statement indicating a specific thing you will be able to do when you have achieved your goal. Objectives are the signposts that tell you when you have reached your goal. They are more concrete and specific than goals. People often identify several objectives to help them define when they've reached their goal.

A goal tells you where you're heading and objectives tell you when you've arrived. You will know you've achieved your goal when you've met your objectives. Before you try to write your own goals and objectives, it may help to see a couple of examples. Let's take a look at what Paul and Susie did.

Paul's Goals and Objectives

You may recall that Paul fears fainting because it will cause him embarrassment. He doesn't totally avoid the subway because it is the only realistic way to get to work, and he will at times catch a bus (after the subway train gets stuck). Paul finds a short bus ride tolerable, but longer ones are more difficult. He also fears long-distance trains and flying. This poses a problem for Paul. His family of origin is in Atlanta, Georgia, and he has not visited them in years. He worries about not seeing his elderly parents again and not being able to go to their funerals.

Paul also fears attending meetings at work (he avoids them sometimes), going to restaurants with people he does not know well, and being called for jury duty. In all these situations, he fears he will be stuck and unable to escape if he feels faint. He would feel terribly embarrassed if he fainted or had to rush anxiously out of a situation to prevent fainting. Paul has two sets of goals and objectives.

Paul's First Goal

I want to be able to use public transportation (subways, buses, trains, and airplanes) comfortably and without restrictions.

Paul's Objectives

- I will use the subway, standing and sitting, and stay in it throughout the trip without carrying my cell phone. I will not drink alcoholic beverages to make me feel better before returning home.

- I will take buses, short and long trips, without escape or use of safety devices.

- I will sometimes take long-distance trains as a part of our vacation.

- I will fly to visit my family and other places and people.

Paul's Second Goal

I want to be able to attend social gatherings with minimal anxiety.

Paul's Objectives

- I will attend all relevant meetings at work.

- I will accept invitations and opportunities to go to restaurants and other social events where I do not know people well.

- I will accept a possible summons to jury duty as a part of my civic duty.

Susie's Goals and Objectives

Recall that Susie fears migraines in public. She feels unable to cope with them and fears that the intense discomfort of the migraine will make her go insane. Since Susie will not leave home alone for more than about fifteen minutes at a time, her life is significantly restricted, reflecting the severity of her agoraphobia. She avoids engaging in the following activities alone: driving or walking more than fifteen minutes from home, driving over bridges, driving to unfamiliar areas, getting into heavy traffic, being a passenger in a car other than when she is with her husband, going to malls, using public transportation, and going to cinemas, restaurants, and parties. Susie has one goal.

Susie's Goal

I want to be able to venture alone far from home by car or foot and engage in any activity I choose, including being in crowded places.

Susie's Objectives

- I will drive about one hour away from home, including over bridges.
- I will drive in unfamiliar areas.
- I will drive in heavy traffic.
- I will be a passenger in a car with other people for up to one hour.
- I will take hour-long walks.
- I will go to malls and stay in them for as long as I want to.
- I will freely use buses and subways.
- I will go to the cinema, restaurants, and parties and attend fundraisers and fairs.

Note that Susie's goal and objectives include some limitations. The reason is that Susie's migraines occur with some frequency and are, at times, quite debilitating. When they're bad, she experiences extreme sensitivity to light and throws up unless she is lying down. Susie also takes powerful medications whenever she feels the onset of a migraine. The medications help, but she doesn't want to get into the habit of taking them more often than necessary.

Susie has decided to err on the side of caution. If, after achieving her initial goal, she discovers that she can handle the headaches well or has fewer of them than expected, she will set a new goal to expand her territory further. She knows that a standstill is not in her best interest.

Under the current circumstances, Susie's goal of traveling one hour away is a big challenge. If she were to have a bad migraine at that distance from home, she might not get home. When planning the actual tasks, she anticipates this and plans what she will do. She carries dark sunglasses to use if needed to block out strong light, and she is prepared to stop the car if she needs to throw up. She will try to reach a rest room but will, in the worst case, throw up on the side of the road. If for some reason she is truly incapacitated, she will call her husband or a friend to take her home. Her public transportation includes buses and subways (relatively short trips), not long-distance trains or airplane flights. If she absolutely needs to, she can leave cinemas, restaurants, parties, or other social events. Instead of anticipating she will be stuck forever and go insane, Susie simpy plans how to deal with the realistic aspects of having a migraine.

Susie's case illustrates the task of sorting out normal precautions from the avoidant coping seen in agoraphobia sufferers. There is nothing wrong with taking measures to ensure safety from real danger or unpleasantness (not driving during a migraine attack) or to reduce severe pain (taking migraine medication).

Developing Your Own Goals and Objectives

Now that you've seen some examples and understand the general issues involved in establishing where you'd like to go, it is time to set your own goals and objectives. Do not rush; it pays to do this well.

Try not to state your goals and objectives merely in terms of feelings (such as "I want to feel less anxious" or "I don't want to have a panic attack"). We know you want to feel better. Your goals and objectives need to include the *specific situations* in which you want to feel more comfortable and the *specific tasks* you want to perform with comfort. This will provide the groundwork for future steps.

Use worksheet 2 to list your goals and objectives, using Paul's and Susie's examples as a model. Begin by identifying your goals. Remember, a goal is a general statement about something you want to accomplish. After you have decided on a particular goal, write out the objectives that will take you to that goal. Remember, objectives are the more specific tasks that define your goal. They tell you when you have achieved your goal.

If you have more than four goals, make more copies of the worksheet. You may want to revisit the list you made in chapter 3, outlining the situations, places, and activities you fear. That list includes situations likely to be difficult for you and should facilitate setting your goals and objectives. You may have one goal for driving, one for walking, and one for doing entertaining activities (going to movies, restaurants, parties, or family get-togethers)

Worksheet 2: Your Goals and Objectives

List your goals and objectives below.   *Check them off as you achieve them.*

Goal # ____ :

_____ ☐

Objectives:

_____ ☐

_____ ☐

_____ ☐

_____ ☐

_____ ☐

_____ ☐

_____ ☐

Goal # ____ :

_____ ☐

Objectives:

_____ ☐

_____ ☐

_____ ☐

_____ ☐

_____ ☐

_____ ☐

_____ ☐

Deciding Where to Begin

If you have only one goal, the direction you will now be heading should be clear. If, however, you have more than one goal, you need to select the one you'll work on first. There is no right or wrong way to do this. The significance of the problem, the level of anxiety generated, and the practical issues involved in completing exposures should all factor in to selecting *your* initial goals.

You may want to start with the goal that addresses the problem that is the most distressing to you or that interferes with your life the most. The advantage here is that you will be addressing something bothersome from the start. People are usually more motivated to solve their most troublesome problems first. They tend to work harder at it. Also, the confidence you acquire should help you grapple with other goals and objectives.

On the other hand, you may decide to start with a goal that addresses a less bothersome issue but is easier to achieve, producing quick success early on. Or, you may decide to start with something that seems the most practical and accessible (for which exposures are easier to arrange) and choose to delay goals that are more complicated to achieve.

Whatever you decide to work on first, make your choice deliberately. If you start with one goal and your situation changes, you can switch to a different goal. Nothing is written in stone. But try to be systematic in your approach and stick with the first goal you choose if you can.

When you've completed worksheet 2, make a copy and keep it handy. You'll be returning to this worksheet again. In chapter 11, you'll need it to help you create your fear hierarchy. You should also use the worksheet whenever the going gets rough, reviewing your goals and objectives to gain motivation. Checking off your objectives on worksheet 2 as you accomplish them will help you recognize your progress and encourage you to continue.

8

Step 2. Acquiring a Healthy Perspective and Useful Coping Strategies

Where We're Going

With your recovery goals and objectives clearly identified, it is time to prepare yourself to confront your fears. In this chapter, you'll learn methods to evaluate and correct your misperceptions of the danger you associate with symptom attacks. You will also learn strategies to cope with anxiety and how to use them effectively.

Perhaps you already feel prepared to face the situations and sensations that make you anxious. Maybe you're eager to get out there and challenge your fears. Slow down! The information and exercises in this chapter are very important and could save you time in the long run. Before you start the exposure work, it will help if you logically understand the difference between what is and is not dangerous, and if you know how to cope with your anxiety in a nonavoidant, adaptive way.

Developing a Healthy Perspective

You need to prepare yourself mentally to face the things that make you anxious. Having a healthy perspective about your fear will help you follow through with what you need to accomplish. A healthy perspective means having an accurate understanding of your fear, even though your emotional brain misjudges your symptom attacks as dangerous. Your logical brain needs to know your fear is irrational. We'll help you distinguish between what you feel and what you intellectually believe will happen in a feared situation.

Consider two people with very different perspectives about their fears. Both are preparing to overcome their fears of panic attacks. Bill believes he will die from a panic attack. He thinks his concerns are reasonable and argues with professionals when they try to correct him. Bill has an unhealthy perspective about his fear. He is not ready to move forward. He is not likely to expose himself to situations he truly believes will kill him. In contrast, Judy has a healthy perspective about her fear. Though she is afraid she may die from a panic attack, she does not actually believe (logically) it will happen. She has learned intellectually that panic attacks cannot make someone die, even though she still fears this might happen. Judy is ready to take the next step. With the proper perspective, she is ready to begin to work on her felt beliefs.

For now, in order to have a healthy perspective about your fear, you must be able to do two things. First, you must know what your feared catastrophe is. You established this in chapter 3. Second, you must be able to identify the errors in your perception of danger.

Identifying the Errors in Your Perception of Danger

By definition, an anxiety *disorder* involves errors in the assessment of danger. Accurate assessments do not lead to dysfunction. It is helpful to know the errors made by your emotional brain that lead you to overpredict danger. Two types of errors are made by people with agoraphobia.

Probability errors. Agoraphobia sufferers tend to exaggerate the likelihood a symptom attack will occur. This is a probability error. Usually, danger signals are relatively poor predictors of symptom attacks, yet people with agoraphobia still perceive them as a sign of imminent danger. For most people with agoraphobia, full-blown attacks occur only a small percentage of the time when the person is in the presence of danger signals. In some cases, sufferers have not had an attack for months or even years.

Severity errors. People with agoraphobia also exaggerate the severity of the consequences of a symptom attack when they are predicting what will happen. This error is based on the belief that catastrophes accompany symptom attacks. Catastrophic outcomes (death, loss of control, incapacitating humiliation) are seen as the likely result of a symptom attack, despite the fact that such outcomes don't occur. Even if agoraphobic individuals do not make a probability error, they almost always exaggerate the severity of what they think will happen if an attack occurs. Very often, they are underestimating their ability to cope.

Your assessment of the danger of symptom attacks probably reflects both types of error. You may overpredict the probability an attack will occur and exaggerate the severity of its consequences if it were to occur. Can you see both of these errors in your perception of danger? (If you would like to read more about general ways of thinking that can lead to errors in judgment about danger, see appendix B.)

Gathering Accurate Information

If you're still not convinced intellectually that your assessment of danger is flawed, you should gather additional information before proceeding to the next section. Remember, you're not likely to do the work necessary to overcome your phobia if you're intellectually unclear or misinformed about the danger of the symptom attack you fear. Here are a few ways to gather additional information relevant to your fear:

1. You can refer to appendix C, in which we provide factual information about the nature and danger of different symptom attacks.

2. You can seek additional information and expert opinion about the symptom attack you fear by reading, surfing the Internet, surveying friends and family, or asking your doctor and other professionals for their input. For example, you can find out if it is common, or even possible, for a headache to make you go crazy, for a panic attack to make you faint, and so on.

3. If your sense of catastrophe involves other people's reactions, you can survey others to find out how they would react to someone throwing up, losing control of their bowels, or any other symptom attack you fear. You will discover that others are not as unforgiving as you may think.

As you seek this information, keep two things in mind. First, no one can guarantee you that the things you fear cannot possibly happen, but other people may be able to give you relevant information about the likelihood of a symptom attack occurring. Even more important, they may inform you about the likelihood of your symptom attack resulting in your feared catastrophe. Second, your goal should be to gather a reasonable amount of information within a reasonable amount of time—not to go from one expert to the next until you're absolutely sure. If you keep gathering until you're 100 percent certain, you'll never move forward. Absolute certainty is not a requirement for action, nor is it even attainable. You need only be reasonably sure.

Useful (Nonavoidant) Coping Strategies

Now that you know what pitfalls to avoid and a general idea of what is required for recovery, you can concentrate on developing effective coping skills. But beware! Many people get confused about what constitutes an effective coping strategy. The purpose of a coping strategy should be to help you stay focused and remain in an anxiety-provoking situation long enough to have a corrective experience. In other words, your strategy should facilitate your attempt to learn through experience that the catastrophe you fear won't occur. Not all ways of coping accomplish this. As you have already learned, safety seeking and other similar ways of coping prevent you from adequately testing your faulty danger predictions.

A useful coping strategy helps you to experience danger signals, not simply get rid of them. It helps you test your belief that symptoms lead to catastrophe. It should not give you the illusion that you have averted a catastrophe. An adaptive coping technique helps you stay in the feared situation and test all the "what ifs" until you are emotionally convinced that the catastrophe you fear is not going to occur.

A common misconception about coping strategies is that they are supposed to relax you. It is simply not realistic to expect to relax while facing a situation you feel is highly threatening. At this point, you may be wondering, "If coping strategies are not supposed to relax you, then what is their purpose? Aren't we supposed to try to control our reactions to things?" Or, "What am I supposed to do? Isn't the ultimate goal to no longer be anxious in these situations?" These are good questions. The ultimate recovery goal is, of course, to be less anxious in the presence of things that currently provoke fear in you. Yet, in order to reach this goal someday, you must discover what truly happens when you are in the presence of things that make you anxious. We know of no effective way for you to do that without you fully facing your danger signals and, with that, anxiety. The road to recovery goes straight through fear.

We have shown you how certain avoidant strategies are invariably not helpful. There are other techniques that can be used properly or improperly. The key to identifying when a technique is appropriate does not lie in the technique itself but in how it is used. Consider diaphragmatic breathing, a coping technique involving the use of slow, deep breaths to reduce arousal. This technique has long been a part of the cognitive behavioral treatment of panic disorder and is still taught by many clinicians, despite the fact that people often misuse diaphragmatic breathing. If you use the technique to try to control your internal danger signals and avoid a panic attack, it can interfere with your ability to change what you believe about the danger of the attack. So, if what you think is, "I have to breathe properly so I don't suffocate and die," you're using the breathing technique as an avoidance strategy. This use of the breathing technique perpetuates your belief that without using it you would have died, which, of course, is not true. If, instead, you use diaphragmatic breathing to help you focus on internal sensations experienced during an exposure or as a way to unwind after an exposure, it can be useful. As you can see, the same technique used in two different ways can produce two very different outcomes.

To summarize, there is no reliable list of techniques that are always useful or always harmful. It depends on how a given technique is used. Therapists are often guilty of teaching techniques such as diaphragmatic breathing and distraction strategies that clients then misuse. In fact, precisely because these techniques are so often misused, well-known treatment centers such as those of Dr. David Barlow in Boston and Dr. David Clark in England no longer teach coping strategies of any kind to clients with agoraphobia and panic disorder.

We agree that eliminating all types of avoidance is necessary for recovery. However, we do not believe that all coping strategies should be eliminated. If used properly, coping strategies can help you successfully complete your exposure work. Once you have adopted a strategy, though, it is paramount that you not let it become another form of avoidance. We will return to this issue in the chapters ahead.

We will now describe some coping strategies that, if used properly, can help you overcome your agoraphobia. Their ultimate utility rests on how you use them. Try them before or during exposure tasks to help you stay in the exposure situation. Be careful not to use them to help you avoid the experience.

Physical and Behavioral Coping Techniques

Some coping strategies are designed to help you manage the physical or behavioral aspects of anxiety. In this section, we describe two of these techniques—diaphragmatic breathing and managing the urge to escape.

Diaphragmatic Breathing

With diaphragmatic breathing, you can affect your physiology. Though breathing is an automatic function of the autonomic nervous system, you can bring aspects of it under voluntary control. This can indirectly help slow down other autonomic nervous system functions, such as your heart rate.

The wonderful thing about diaphragmatic breathing is that it is a natural relaxant. When you become anxious, you naturally tend to breathe faster and more shallowly. At times, your body is so aroused that it becomes hard to concentrate. When you use diaphragmatic breathing, you should use it to stay focused on your sensations. You can thus lower your arousal and then proceed to challenge your catastrophic thinking. Later, you can do the challenging without diaphragmatic breathing! This way you'll know you are not using it as an avoidant mechanism.

When it is helpful, when it is not. As we've said, diaphragmatic breathing can be applied in helpful or detrimental ways. Here are some further hints on how to determine when it is useful and when it isn't. Diaphragmatic breathing can be helpful in the following situations:

- If you are getting ready to do an exposure and feel anxious, you might want to do the breathing to be more centered before you start the exposure.

- When you have completed and exposure, but your body is still tense, you can use the breathing to slow your body down.

- Diaphragmatic breathing is useful if you have a medical condition that requires you to limit your arousal.

- If the breathing helps you focus on your symptoms and the exposure experience.

Diaphragmatic breathing is not helpful in these situations:

- If you use it to try to avoid a symptom attack that is not dangerous.

- During a panic attack when you feel fear. (After your fear has subsided, you can do diaphragmatic breathing simply to lower your physical arousal.)

How to Learn Diaphragmatic Breathing

Instructions: Practice one step at a time. Do not proceed to the next step until you have mastered the previous one. Make sure that you practice five minutes, twice a day. Practice daily for a couple of weeks or longer, if necessary.

1. Lie on your back on a bed or carpeted floor. If you can, do it without a pillow under your head. Instead of placing a pillow there, place two or three pillows on your stomach/diaphragm. Keep your head against the mattress or carpet. Breathe in and out deeply. As you breathe in, your diaphragm/stomach should expand (to allow for the extra air), thus raising the pillows. As you breathe out, the pillows should come back down again. It is good to exaggerate the movement of your diaphragm, especially while learning the technique. Breathe slowly *in and out through your nose*, not through your mouth (unless you have a bad cold, asthma, or something obstructing your nasal passages).

2. Lie on your back as above, but get rid of the pillows and place your hand over your navel. Look at the ceiling or close your eyes. Proceed as before. This time feel with your hand as your stomach rises up and down.

3. Lie on your back as above, with your arms at your sides. Look at the ceiling or close your eyes. Proceed to breathe as before. This time place your *mind* on your diaphragm/stomach and feel it move up and down (become one with your breathing).

4. Sit on a sofa or couch, slouching back, so that you can watch your stomach area. Watch your diaphragm/stomach move up as you breathe in, down as you breathe out.

5. Sit straight up, doing the same. Make sure that your upper chest and shoulders are perfectly still.

6. Stand up and do the same.

7. Once you have mastered the above steps, start paying attention to your breathing during the day while sitting at work, watching TV, and so on. The more you do this, the better. Once you have learned it well, you can start to apply it when you are anxious.

- If you rarely ever vomit, have diarrhea, lose control of your bladder, or suffer from migraines.

If you want to learn diaphragmatic breathing, we recommend that you proceed in the order outlined in the preceding instructions. You'll find that practicing first while lying down is the best way to learn the technique. (For information on the physiology and symptoms of hyperventilation, see appendix D).

Managing the Urge to Escape

If you leave a situation because of anxiety, you are *escaping*. If you leave a situation according to a preset plan, you are *exiting*. In agoraphobia, the fear of entrapment is paramount: you believe you are unable to leave because of physical or social constraints. Do you feel trapped standing in line, in cinemas or theaters (especially if in the middle of a row), malls, stores, classrooms, restaurants, parties, buses, streetcars, or freeways? The sense of entrapment is usually psychological, not physical. In reality, you can physically leave most situations. You need to discover that you can, and exercise the freedom to do so. Experimenting with the exposure is more important than completing the action. (You must, of course, use good judgment when leaving so that you do not jeopardize your job, a class [taking a test], and so on.)

You can plan to make an exit from the places you fear. You can plan in advance on leaving five, fifteen, or thirty minutes after your arrival, depending on the situation. When it comes to freeways, you can determine to exit after a certain number of exits. Watch the time or number of exits and then *leave*. If you plan to leave and *don't* leave, then you are falling back on your old strategy of planning escape routes. Here we ask you to actually carry out your plan. For instance, if you fear sitting in a movie theater throughout the movie, plan on leaving the movie after fifteen minutes, making sure that you leave then. You can plan to go to the cinema on another day for thirty minutes; soon you will be able to stay for the entire time.

One client with an upcoming flight to Europe complained of feeling trapped on airplanes. She said that if she sat in the middle of a row and needed to use the rest room while other passengers had food trays in front of them, she would feel totally trapped. Even here, we devised a planned exit for her to discover that she was not really trapped. In this instance, she was to apologetically excuse herself, saying that she had to get up right then. And although this would be terribly inconvenient for other people, they would pick up their trays and stand up, or ask others to hold the trays so that they could move out of the way, in order to let her out. As it was, she did not actually carry out this particular exposure, but the issue was gone once she realized that even in this circumstance she would have a little freedom.

Occasionally, people escape before they plan to leave because of unexpectedly high anxiety. Here you can practice trying to stay in a situation a little longer, preferably until after your anxiety has diminished some. Most importantly, if you leave a situation because of anxiety, you must seek out that exposure *as soon as possible* again. Preferably you will return to the situation a few minutes later. At least try to return the next day. If you escape in the middle of high anxiety without returning, your fear may grow.

Mental Coping Techniques

Other coping strategies are designed to manage the mental aspects of anxiety. In this section, we cover three of these techniques—objectively describing your anxiety symptoms, realistically assessing what you can control, and using corrective coping statements.

Objectively Describing Your Anxiety Sensations

The first mental coping technique has to do with staying in the here and now. A number of meditation techniques are about anchoring yourself in breathing and learning to focus and live in the here and now. *Mindfulness meditation* accomplishes this. We recommend two books by Jon Kabat- Zinn, *Full Catastrophe Living: Using the Wisdom of Your Body and Mind to Face Stress, Pain, and Illness* (1990) and *Wherever You Go, There You Are: Mindfulness Meditation in Everyday Life* (1994). They discuss this approach in more detail.

It's important that you do not say to yourself, "Oh no! I'm having a panic attack! I can't stand it!" Instead, try describing exactly what you notice. For instance, "I'm feeling quite light-headed and tingly. Nothing else is occurring." Or, "I'm thinking again that I'll have a diarrhea attack, but so far I only have some mild intestinal sensations. If I need to go to the bathroom later, I will, but I do not need to now." Or, "I'm driving well, paying attention to my car and the traffic." Or, "My heart is beating fast, I feel some numbness in my arm, and I feel dizzy and a little disoriented."

No matter how well you prepare yourself for an exposure, you will feel discomfort, anxiety, and even at times a symptom attack. But you can be prepared for it. You do not have to let it take you totally by surprise. *When you feel it, it does not mean you've failed.* Forget projecting into the future by asking yourself, "What if _____ will happen?" but stay in the here and now. Ask yourself, "What is actually taking place right now?"

You can observe and describe your sensations, behavior, and surroundings objectively, without judgment. You can say, "Even though my heart is racing, I feel numbness in my hands and feet, and I have these feelings of unreality, I am *maintaining my behavior.* In spite of the sensations, I am holding onto the steering wheel, pressing the gas pedal, and watching where I am going." Or, "Nothing terrible is happening on this freeway right now. The traffic is as it should be." Staying in the here and now is a very powerful coping mechanism.

Realistically Assessing What You Can Control

You can make anxiety work for or against you. You need to accept the reality that many things are not under your control. Otherwise, you will feel anxious every time you encounter situations you don't control. On the other hand, it behooves you to control what you can. It is similar to the sense of entrapment. As much as people with agoraphobia want control and freedom, they often focus on the opposite. Bear with us as we explain how this occurs.

Accept what you can and cannot control. When you scrutinize your environment, focusing on every way you do *not* have control instead of every way you *do* have control, you become more fearful. You may say, "There are too many people here," instead of, "Even if there are lots of people here, I can still get around. These people are not bothering me. In fact, they seem friendly or neutral."

Give up trying to control how you feel. The more you try to control anxiety and panic, the less control you actually have. This is because the more energy you expend, the more anxiety gets generated. Paradoxically, if you yield to anxiety and panic—let them alone—you ultimately have more control.

Give up trying to control the outside world. It is important to recognize that many things in your environment are not in your control. The more you accept this as a reality of life, the better off you are. It is better to put your energy into things you can control and not into things you can't control. For example, you cannot control how other people behave, but you can control how you deal with their behavior.

Dismantle false perceptions of entrapment. Instead of looking for every way you think you're trapped, look for every way you're *not* trapped. You can get out of most situations, some sooner, some later. Take the example of being in a movie theater. Most people usually do not feel trapped in movie theaters; they know they can leave any time they wish. In contrast, many people with agoraphobia feel they cannot possibly leave. They usually fear that their departure will convey their anxiety. In fact, it doesn't. The truth is, no one pays attention to why someone else exits from a movie theater. People leave for all kinds of reasons: they need to go to the bathroom, their cell phone rings, or they find the movie boring.

In many situations, *you may choose to be confined for a while,* such as in a dentist's chair, on the subway, or on an airplane. Being there is a means to an end. At the same time, in your mind you can be as free as you want to be. On an airplane, you can fully immerse yourself in a novel or in the image of being on a beach in Hawaii.

We are not suggesting these coping methods as safety behaviors or escapes, but to demonstrate what the average person does. Other people are just as confined as you are in these circumstances, but they do not perceive themselves as being trapped. Also, remember, if there is no realistic danger, there is nothing from which you need to escape.

Using Corrective Coping Statements

There are statements you can make to yourself that will help you face your fears, without providing false reassurance. We call these *corrective coping statements*. Such statements should alter your inaccurate perception of danger, but they must also be realistic. For example, the phrase, "I'll never throw up," is not realistic and it promotes avoidance. A more useful and realistic statement is, "I can handle it if someone disapproves of me throwing up." This statement corrects the prediction that you'll be overwhelmed by and incapable of coping with the experience of vomiting in front of others. You can repeat the corrective coping phrase over and over in your mind, or you can carry a card with you with the phrase written on it, to refer to when you are concerned.

Here are the characteristics of a good corrective coping statement. A useful (nonavoidant) statement should be:

- *Brief.* A sentence or two should do it. You want something you can easily remember.

- *Realistic.* Basically, the statement should be true—something that will be born of your experience. "I will not be anxious" is not realistic. "I will handle my anxiety" is realistic.

- *Corrective.* The statement should correct the errors in your perception of danger. If your fear is that you'll get light-headed, pass out, and become incapacitated by embarrassment, then a corrective coping statement would be, "It's unlikely I'll faint, but I can cope with it if I do."

Are You Ready?

We're almost ready to start your exposure work. In the upcoming chapters, we plan to use all of the principles covered so far to help you deal more comfortably and effectively with situations that now create anxiety for you. But before we begin, we need to ask you some important questions.

Are you able to see how you think differently from the average person about the situations you fear? At least intellectually (that is, in your rational mind), are you clear that you overpredict danger? Do you understand (logically) that your fear is irrational? Do you understand how your catastrophic thinking and avoidance fuel your phobia? For instance, do you know that anxiety-related heart palpitations do not lead to heart attacks? Do you know that a sensation of shortness of breath does not actually mean you will suffocate to death? Do you know that anxiety, which slightly raises blood pressure, does not lead to fainting (which instead results from a sudden, significant *drop* in blood pressure)? Do you know that getting upset and having jumbled thoughts does not actually lead to insanity? Do you believe, again intellectually, that people around you are not watching your every move, ready to judge you for a transgression, such as showing signs of anxiety? Or if someone did, would it matter?

It is essential that you believe intellectually that a symptom attack will not lead to catastrophe. Otherwise, you will not benefit from this self-help program.

Here are some steps you may want to consider if you are still in doubt:

- See a physician again. Do you need more tests done in order to be convinced that you're physically healthy?

- Ask several people you know if they have ever had the symptoms you're concerned about, and if they share your concerns. For example, have they ever felt short of breath and, if so, do they believe they could die from the sensation?

- Seek an evaluation from a mental-health professional to clarify your mental status and convince you that you will not go crazy.

- Go through this book again from the beginning in an attempt to gain deeper understanding and knowledge.

Ultimately, you are the best judge to determine what you must do to be convinced of what we are saying. If you cannot find a way to convince yourself and you really believe that your danger signals equal real danger, then you need to seek professional help for your agoraphobia. Only having reached a rational insight can you benefit from the program in this book. Only then will exposure help you change your felt belief.

If you are ready, proceed to chapter 9, where you'll learn to restructure your beliefs about danger.

9

Step 3. Challenging Your Felt Beliefs about Danger

Where We're Going

In this chapter, you'll learn how to challenge your felt beliefs as you begin to face the things you fear in a systematic way. To bridge the gap from knowledge to exposure practices, you'll learn to use a new tool that will help you challenge your fears directly and repeatedly. Doing so will go hand in hand with your ongoing exposure work.

Having come this far, you are aware of the errors in your perception of danger and may logically understand that your feared symptom attack does not result in catastrophe. Yet as you know, knowledge and insight do not automatically translate into behavioral and emotional change. You'll be making a big jump from insight to practice. This will not be easy. You will have to approach uncomfortable situations that you may have been avoiding for quite some time. And we will be instructing you to do this in a way that, at first, will probably feel riskier than the way you have done things in the past. But being willing to do what feels risky is necessary to change your beliefs about danger. And actively challenging your felt beliefs is an important part of this process.

Restructuring Felt Beliefs

We have discussed the difference between logical and felt beliefs. You can gain insight from the factual information you gather about symptom attacks, and your logical beliefs can become more realistic, but to achieve a change in your felt beliefs is another story. Through past experience, you know your felt beliefs can be stubborn and, thus, difficult to change. That is why it is so important to challenge them repeatedly, especially while you are in the situations you fear. We begin the process of challenging your felt beliefs in this chapter.

It is true that it takes changes in action—behavioral work—to overcome phobias. This behavioral work helps produce changes in the emotional mind in a way that logic and factual information cannot. Yet ultimately, cognitive change must take place along with behavioral and emotional change in order for fear to diminish permanently. In other words, to be free of your phobia, you must ultimately think, feel, and behave as if the symptom attack is not dangerous. The experiential learning you'll go through in chapters 10 and 11, aided by a continued effort to challenge your felt beliefs about danger, is the best way to reduce your fear of symptom attacks.

If you work with your mind constructively, you can greatly facilitate the exposure work you'll be doing. Again, negative self-statements are detrimental for exposure. It does not help if you're saying things like, "I can't wait until this is over. This is awful," or "I don't know if I can cope with this." That is why we recommend using positive coping statements. They can help you stay in the situation and focus on the experience. An example would be, "I can handle my anxiety." But even this kind of mental strategy has limitations. It does not adequately address the faulty belief system behind your fear. To overcome your phobia, you must ultimately change your fear structure.

Challenging Your Felt Beliefs

It takes work to reprogram your mind; you need to challenge your beliefs at a deeper level. Worksheet 3: Challenging Felt Beliefs shows how to do so. With the help of this worksheet, you'll state exactly what triggers your fears and you'll challenge the faulty beliefs underlying them. You will come up with alternative ways of looking at your triggers and symptom attacks.

Initially, your felt beliefs may resist alternative perspectives. But the more you practice with this worksheet, the more easily new ways of thinking will come. You'll learn to actively challenge your fears in situations that provoke them. The goal is thus to achieve a change in your fear structure, what we call *cognitive restructuring,* where your beliefs about danger change to nondanger. This worksheet alone will not change your fear structure—to do so requires exposure to the situations you fear—but it can help.

This worksheet is a wonderful tool to use *before* an anticipated exposure to help you identify exactly what fears you are faced with. While this will not eliminate your fear, it may make it easier to challenge your fear during the exposure.

You can also use the worksheet *during* exposures, at least in situations where it is practical for you to write (such as when you feel anxious sitting in a classroom). It may help you focus on the experience. The earlier you intervene by challenging your fears, the greater the impact.

You can, of course, also use the worksheet right *after* exposures. If you do the worksheet after an exposure, however, do it quickly thereafter. If you wait more than a day, you may not recall each step as accurately. And the process of challenging your fear loses its connection to the actual exposure.

As you do the worksheet over and over, you'll learn how to use it by heart. Make at least ten copies of the worksheet because it takes using this tool about that number of times or more before you can memorize it. The point is to complete enough worksheets that you become able to follow the steps in your head. The ultimate goal is to be able to use this method wherever you are without having to write anything down. Remember, challenging your beliefs is one of the most helpful ways to cope with a feared situation, as long as you are doing so in a realistic fashion.

How to Use Worksheet 3

We pointed out how important it is to state the *specific aspects of your fear.* Using worksheet 3, you'll record external danger signals (situations), exact internal danger signals (sensations), feared symptom attacks, and finally, feared catastrophes. As you use the worksheet, try to be as specific as possible. If your feared symptom attack is panic, break it down into the specific sensation or sensations that scare you.

Your ultimate threat is a feared catastrophe. This is what you'll be challenging in the worksheet. You'll write down your evidence (why you think the catastrophe will happen), whether or not it is logical, then you'll directly refute the evidence based on experience or logic, and finally you'll look for alternative evidence or explanations. This means that you will be looking for alternative ways to explain the events you fear. In the case of social threat, there is one additional small step. You'll need to rethink how serious it truly would be if someone were to reject you. Most people would not relish feeling rejected, but they do not see it as a catastrophe. We want you to learn to respond in a similar fashion.

Before trying to do your own worksheet, you'll benefit greatly from looking at the examples of Paul and Susie. (Refer to chapter 7 to review their different fears.) Looking at these examples, ask yourself how Paul and Susie came to conclude that their catastrophic fear would take place. As you can see, the evidence does not have to be logical. The actual challenge starts with refuting the evidence and coming up with alternative ways to explain events. Note that if Susie truly had a bad migraine, her alternative plan to put on dark glasses, take medication, and sit down on a bench to see if the migraine improves would not constitute escape or use of safety devices. It would be coping. If Susie just *thought she might* get a migraine and did the same things all the time (just in cast), then she would be engaging in escape and use of safety devices. Also note that fainting was not Paul's ultimate catastrophic fear. His catastrophic fear was really being overcome with embarrassment.

In the upcoming chapters, you'll be using the worksheet as you do your exposures to feared situations. The worksheet begins with a place to put the date. This is because you can only challenge *one current event* at a time. If you make many driving exposures, you may experience the same fears time and again. Yet you should do a new worksheet with each exposure, even if the worksheets end up looking almost identical. Repeating the worksheet is important. You can continue to do it until you conquer your fears.

Paul's Worksheet 3:
Challenging Felt Beliefs

1. **Date:** *5-3-03.*

2. **External Danger Signal** (Write down the specific situation that makes you anxious):

   At a restaurant for a work retirement party. Coworkers and their spouses are attending.

3. **Internal Danger Signal** (Write down the specific sensations that make you anxious):

   Dry mouth and a "spacy" feeling.

4. **Feared Symptom Attack** (If panic, specify what sensations in the panic scare you):

   A panic attack with light-headedness and feelings of unreality.

5. **Feared Catastrophe** (Write down the exact thing, i.e., the worst thing, that you think will happen):

   I will faint, feel totally embarrassed, and be unable to cope.

6. **Challenging the Threat**

Your evidence: Why you think the catastrophic fear will happen; does not have to be logical.

   People get scared when they see someone faint; that is so embarrassing!

Then refute! Counter your evidence using your own or other people's past experience or logic.

   I've asked my close friends what they'd think if they saw someone faint. They said they'd try to help and see what's wrong.

Alternatives: Can the sensations/the event have another explanation or lead to something harmless?

   I will most likely not faint. If I were to faint for some reason, people will be concerned and try to help me

So, what if? If your fear is social threat, and you truly were rejected, what would happen?

   If someone made fun of me for fainting, they'd be rude! I can live with that. Or they may just want to make light of the situation; that's okay.

Susie's Worksheet 3:
Challenging Felt Beliefs

1. **Date:** *6-18-03.*

2. **External Danger Signal** (Write down the specific situation that makes you anxious):

   Alone in the mall for 2 hours.

3. **Internal Danger Signal** (Write down the specific sensations that make you anxious):

   I feel spots in my eyes, neck pain, migraine aura.

4. **Feared Symptom Attack** (If panic, specify what sensations in the panic scare you):

   A migraine headache.

5. **Feared Catastrophe** (Write down the exact thing, i.e., the worst thing, that you think will happen):

   I will get a migraine, feel totally unable to cope, and go insane.

6. **Challenging the Threat**

Your evidence: Why you think the catastrophic fear will happen; does not have to be logical.

> *I do get very bad migraines, sometimes vomiting if I am not lying down. I feel dysfunctional. If I have to endure this in public, it will get so bad I'll lose my mind and go insane.*

Then refute! Counter your evidence using your own or other people's past experience or logic.

> *I have not always been in bed with a bad migraine. Sometimes I had to take care of the children and even though it felt torturous, I did not go insane.*

Alternatives: Can the sensations/the event have another explanation or lead to something harmless?

> *I may not get a migraine or get only a very mild one. If the migraine bothered me a lot, I could put on my dark glasses, take the medication, and sit down on a bench to see if it got better. If truly bad, I could leave. I could probably drive home slowly; if not, I'll take a cab.*

So, what if? If your fear is social threat and you truly were rejected, what would happen?

Worksheet 3:
Challenging Felt Beliefs

1. **Date:**

2. **External Danger Signal** (Write down the specific situation that makes you anxious):

3. **Internal Danger Signal** (Write down the specific sensations that make you anxious):

4. **Feared Symptom Attack** (If panic, specify what sensations in the panic scare you):

5. **Feared Catastrophe** (Write down the exact thing, i.e., the worst thing, that you think will happen):

6. **Challenging the Threat**

Your evidence: Why you think the catastrophic fear will happen; does not have to be logical.

Then refute! Counter your evidence using your own or other people's past experience or logic.

Alternatives: Can the sensations/the event have another explanation or lead to something harmless?

So, what if? If your fear is social threat, and you truly were rejected, what would happen?

10

Step 4. Overcoming Your Fear of Internal Sensations in the Absence of External Danger Signals

Where We're Going

With a clear path set to reach your goal, it is now time to begin your exposure work. The next step is to overcome your fear of internal sensations. Why is this so important? Because you will never be fully free of agoraphobia unless you learn to trust that the sensations that make you anxious, no matter how uncomfortable, are actually harmless. In this chapter, we will begin this process, known as interoceptive exposure. The first exposure task is to become less afraid of internal sensations in an environment you perceive as relatively safe, that is, one without external danger signals. We'll deal with external danger signals in chapter 11.

From reading the previous chapters in this book, you know what is needed to overcome agoraphobia: systematic exposure to internal *and* external danger signals. Until the mid-1980s, agoraphobia treatment focused on in vivo exposure to external danger signals. But many people who received this treatment still feared symptom attacks. Only later did most of us recognize that agoraphobics are afraid of external danger signals in part because of the presence of internal danger signals. Researchers and clinicians then set out to develop procedures to help people become less afraid of their internal sensations. These procedures were given a technical term: "interoceptive exposure." Interoception refers to sensory feedback from within your body (heartbeat, breathing irregularities, faint feelings, gastrointestinal distress, nausea, and so on). The early results of interoceptive exposure were promising, and therapists were hopeful that this procedure alone might be sufficient to treat agoraphobia. Many of us thought in vivo exposure might no longer be necessary. Lo and behold, we were proven wrong! Experience and research showed that in vivo exposure is still necessary to treat agoraphobia completely. Hence, the twofold approach: dealing with internal sensations and external situations. You need both interoceptive and in vivo exposures to deal with internal as well as external danger signals. This combined approach gives you the best chance for recovery from agoraphobia.

How Does Interoceptive Exposure Work?

In chapter 3, you checked off the sensations that scare you. You learned that you interpret these sensations as signs of danger, as indicators of an impending symptom attack. In chapter 2, we described how this fear develops. Once a person becomes fearful of an internal sensation, the fear persists and does not easily go away. You may logically know that the things you fear are not dangerous, but fear hangs on stubbornly. For this reason, it is necessary to expose yourself to internal sensations (internal danger signals). Here, we will guide you through interoceptive exposure so that you can systematically experience the internal sensations that currently make you anxious. By provoking these sensations on purpose and allowing yourself to experience them without avoidance, you will learn that they are not dangerous.

You can move through this program at your own pace, one step at a time. First, you'll create mild levels of these sensations. Then gradually, as you feel ready, you'll make them more intense. We'll begin by working on these sensations in nonthreatening places. You can start provoking them at home, and later in other places, as you feel more capable. The exposure needs to be repeated again and again. This allows you eventually to become comfortable with internal danger signals.

Choosing What Sensations to Work On

You will find a list of exercises in table 10.1 at the end of the chapter, along with worksheet 4, in which you will record your exposures. Each sensation has a specific exercise designed to provoke it. However, every person's mind and body are unique. Since people fear a variety of sensations, we do not expect you to practice all the exercises in table 10.1. That would be a waste of time. You should only practice those exercises relevant to your internal danger signals. We will do our best to guide you to the most relevant exercises.

We specify the amount of time to do each exercise, though there is nothing magical about the time limits. (Most of the exercises bring on sensations quickly. Others take a while.) In some cases, an exercise will not bring on the expected sensation. If this happens to you, you should always ask yourself whether or not you did the exercise correctly or long enough. If no expected effects occur, try reading the instructions again. If you are doing the exercise correctly and still not producing the intended sensation, then try it for a little longer (in the case of producing hyperventilation, about thirty seconds longer). Another good plan is to ask someone else to read the instructions and try out the exercise so that you can observe how that person interprets and applies the instructions.

You will create your own interoceptive exposure profile by choosing items from the list of interoceptive exercises in table 10.1 that cover *all* your feared sensations. This is similar to what you'll do with exposures to external situations in chapter 11. Sensations that do not scare you are irrelevant. Performing exercises related to those sensations will not benefit you. However, it may be helpful to glance over the descriptions of all the exercises in the table, especially if the ones you picked don't create any anxiety. See if you think any of the other ones might work. You could even do a trial run. When we do the exercises with clients, we find that some exercises bring on sensations that were not expected. If the exercises do not fully create a feared sensation, we encourage you to be creative. Can you think of a good exercise to bring on relevant sensations not listed here? Anything inherently safe and practical is fair game. The important thing is to create relevant exposures.

A Cautionary Note

None of the exercises outlined in this book are dangerous if you are healthy. They are, in fact, quite harmless. However, some of the exercises could possibly exacerbate certain medical conditions, if you have them. You should consult your physician before proceeding with this part of the program, especially if you have not had a physical examination in the past six months.

You will need to avoid some of the exercises if you have any of the following medical conditions or illnesses:

- epilepsy or other history of seizures

- moderate to severe asthma

- chronic arrhythmia or fibrillations

- heart or lung problems

- history of fainting or *very low* blood pressure

- pregnancy

To give you an idea, if you have seizures, you should definitely not hyperventilate or look at dotted or checkered surfaces. If you have moderate-to-severe asthma, you should avoid hyperventilation or breathing through a thin straw. If you have vertigo or another balance problem, spinning while standing is not recommended. If you are pregnant, you should avoid a number of the exercises. Use common sense. If you have a very bad back, you may not want to spin while standing, but you might be able to spin while seated in a chair. The above list is not comprehensive. You may have another condition that shouldn't be combined with these exercises.

To be on the safe side, if you have a medical condition or have any concerns at all about an exercise, ask your physician. Bring this book along on your next visit and show your doctor the exercises you'll be doing. Your physician should be able to advise you.

Carrying Out Your Interoceptive Exposures

Before beginning these exercises, you will need to decide where to do them, and you will need to collect a few items. You will also need to learn how to rate the intensity of your internal responses to these exercises.

Where to Do the Exercises

Most often, people choose to do the exercises at home at first. Remember what you are trying to accomplish. The external situation should feel relatively safe, and home is safe for most people. Since you need to concentrate on the sensation without distractions, choose and create the right conditions. Do not do the exercises while watching TV, talking to family members (including children), listening to the radio, and so on. There are reasons to do some of the procedures in settings other than your home, but choose situations you perceive as nonthreatening. Later you will try doing the exercises in other places.

Items You Will Need

You will need a few things. Make sure you have these items whenever you start an exercise:

1. A timer. You want a timer that rings when the time is up. (Do not use a watch or clock that you will have to stop to look at; this would be too distracting in most exercises. It is also not good to monitor the time too closely. Concentrate on your exercise, and let the timer tell you when the time is up.)

2. A pen and Worksheet 4: Your Daily Interoceptive Exposure Log (at the end of this chapter). You will need two to four copies.

3. There are a few other items you may need, depending on the exercise. For example, coffee stirrers or cocktail straws are needed for one of the procedures. The description of each exercise will indicate what additional items you will need.

Rating the Intensity of the Sensations and Your Anxiety

From working with many individuals with anxiety disorders, we have observed that some people confuse physical discomfort with anxiety. As anxiety takes over an increasingly greater part of your life, you learn to interpret any discomfort as anxiety. Instead of noticing sadness, anger, despair, disappointment, pain, utter fatigue, or light-headedness, you feel anxiety. This is not a healthy development because your experience of anxiety increases at the expense of other feelings. All you notice is anxiety. It is healthy to be able to experience a great variety of emotions and physical sensations, the way other people do. A simple example would be a headache. Most people think of a strong headache as being intensely uncomfortable, but getting a headache does not produce fear.

Being able to tell the difference between various feelings or symptoms is particularly helpful for interoceptive exposure. We want you to be able to distinguish between the intensity of two responses—the physical sensation you're trying to provoke and the anxiety that accompanies it. Making this distinction is important because the two responses are not inevitably tied together. Over time, you can expect the intensity of your anxiety to diminish in response to a particular interoceptive exposure. This is because you will have become less afraid of the sensation. However, the intensity of the physical sensation that is provoked by the exposure should not change significantly. Spinning, for example, consistently creates dizziness, but only creates anxiety in those who are afraid spinning will lead to a catastrophe.

When you embark on an exercise, pay attention to the intensity of the sensation and any anxiety associated with it. Learn to distinguish between the two. Using worksheet 4, rate the intensity of the sensation (how strong the sensation is) along a sensation intensity scale from 0 to 10 (0 indicating no sensation at all and 10 indicating an overwhelmingly strong sensation). Rate your level of anxiety along an anxiety level scale, also from 0 to 10 (where 0 indicates no anxiety at all and 10 indicates overwhelming anxiety or absolute panic).

Ultimately, we want you to be able to experience a strong sensation with little or no anxiety. That is the goal of interoceptive exposure. As therapists, we have done these exercises many times over with new clients and know from experience that the intensity of the sensation remains high for many of the exercises, no matter how many times you do them. The point is not to diminish the sensation but to *feel it fully and learn not to fear it.*

Two Examples of Interoceptive Exposure

Before you begin your own interoceptive exposures, first look at what Paul and Susie experience. Everyone's situation is different, but it may help you get a feel for the process.

Paul's Experience

Refer to Paul's worksheet 3 in chapter 9. His feared symptom attack was panic with sensations of light-headedness and feelings of unreality. His internal danger signals varied (as precursors of a panic attack) but he described them mainly as feeling "spacy." His feared catastrophe was fainting in public situations and being incapacitated by humiliation. The interoceptive exercises he chose were placing his head between his legs, spinning, and hyperventilation (see table 10.1).

First he addressed the erroneous hypothesis that panic symptoms of light-headedness and unreality would lead to fainting. He practiced daily at home, placing his head between his legs and sitting back up quickly. He also practiced spinning and hyperventilation. He found that placing his head between his legs produced a sensation intensity of 3 and an anxiety level of 2. After one more trial, his sensation intensity went to 2 and anxiety level to 0. Spinning did not make him faint. However, it produced a sensation intensity of 6 and an anxiety level of 2 the first time. The second time around, the sensation intensity was still 6 and anxiety level 1. The anxiety levels in these exercises were low to begin with and quickly dropped down. It was different with hyperventilation, which produced a sensation intensity of 8 and an anxiety level of 7. He worked on hyperventilation daily for two weeks. While his sensation intensity remained at 8, his anxiety level eventually dropped to 1.

Susie's Experience

Refer to Susie's worksheet 3 in chapter 9. Susie's feared symptom attack was having a migraine. Her feared catastrophe was that a migraine would lead to the inability to cope, resulting in insanity. Her internal danger signals were spots in her visual field, neck pain, and migraine aura. She worked on the following interoceptive exercises: staring at a page of dots, using imagery to picture herself being in an insane asylum, and watching movies and reading biographies about people who have gone insane. She did this over a period of four weeks, since it involved reading and watching movies. In the beginning, the anxiety level for imagining being in an insane asylum was a 9, and reading books on insane people was a 7. At the end of the four weeks, the levels dropped to 3 and 2, respectively. At this point, she decided to write in detail about how she might end up in an insane asylum, which she repeated six times. At the end of these exercises, her anxiety level dropped to 1. She learned that imagining these things did not make them happen.

Doing Your Exercises Using Table 10.1

Table 10.1 depicts a list of feared sensations. For each one, it gives exercises to work on with detailed instructions. First, look over the list carefully. Find the sensation or symptom attack that you fear, and write down all the exercises you need to work on in the area provided at the end the table. If your list turns out to be incomplete, you can add more exercises later.

General instructions: Once you are ready to do an exercise, read the specific instructions carefully. In each case, after you have created a desired sensation, *focus your full attention on that sensation.* Don't distract yourself or try to get rid of the sensation. There is no set amount of time you must experience a particular sensation; rather, the important thing is to stay focused on the sensation *until your anxiety diminishes in the presence of the sensation.* If the sensation goes away before your anxiety has had a chance to decrease, you need to repeat the exercise. If the minimum amount of time recommended for an exercise is too difficult, you can cut it back to a level that feels manageable and increase it later.

Once an exercise produces little or no anxiety, you're ready to increase the intensity of the exercise (for example, more minutes jogging in place, drinking another cup of coffee, and so on) or move on to another exercise, if needed. Use worksheet 4 at the end of this chapter to record your experiences with each exercise.

Table: 10.1 Interoceptive Exercises

Feared Sensations

Exercise	*Instructions*
Heart Palpitations	
Running in place	Jog in place for one minute. Jog vigorously. Or run up stairs. If needed, build up the time until your heart beats fast, as happens with a good workout.
Doing step-ups	Using a staircase, take one step up, one down, one up, one down, alternating legs. Do this for a minute and a half. Lengthen the time as needed for a good workout.
Using a squat machine in gym	Start with one minute; build up as needed for a good workout.
Ingesting caffeine	Drink one cup of caffeinated coffee or tea (rather strong). Then practice with two cups.
Dizziness/Light-headedness/Faint Feelings	
Putting head between legs	Sit in a straight chair. Bend your head down between your legs, trying to keep it lower than your heart level. Set the timer for one and a half minutes. When the timer goes off, *quickly* lift your head and stare straight ahead for a little while.
Spinning	Spin around at a good pace for one minute. Give yourself room and have a wall nearby to put your hand against if you lose your balance. Then do it again for one minute and immediately walk with the dizzy feelings. If you're so off balance that you may fall, practice several times without walking, then with walking. Or use an office chair that spins and push against the floor as you spin.

Hyperventilating	While *standing,* breathe deeply in and out through your *mouth* (like panting, but a bit slower). Emphasize the out breath, making an audible sound that can be heard across the room as you exhale. Do this for one and a half minutes. If the sensations are not very strong, build up to two minutes, even up to three. (If done right, people seldom need a full three minutes to feel strong sensations.)

Shortness of Breath/Sensation of Difficulty Breathing/Sense of Suffocation

Hyperventilating	See previous instructions.
Straw breathing	Place a thin straw in your mouth and breathe in and out only through the straw. Do this for two minutes. Next, do the same while also *slightly* pinching the nose with your other hand. (Use *thin* straws. We use a straw that has a three-millimeter inside diameter. Larger straws would defeat the purpose. It has to be challenging.)
Putting pillow over face	Lie on the bed and place a pillow *loosely* over your face. Make sure no one in the family will play tricks on you, pressing down on the pillow. Do this for one minute, then build up to two minutes.
Sitting in a dark, tight closet, with door closed	For this to work, the fit must be truly tight, with lots of clothes in it. Keep the door closed. You can sit on a stool. Start with five minutes and build up to fifteen minutes.
Lying under bed	Lie on your back under the bed or lie on your stomach. It needs to be a pretty tight fit. Do this for one minute and build up to five minutes.
Wearing tight clothing around neck	Wear something tight around your neck; a collar, scarf, or turtleneck sweater. Start with thirty minutes and build up to one hour.
Wearing a dust mask	Cover your nose and mouth with the mask and breathe in and out. Start with fifteen minutes and build up to half an hour.

Feeling Warm or Hot/Sense of Suffocation

Creating heat	Turn up the heat in the house and wear very warm clothing. Do so for fifteen minutes, then

build up to thirty. Alternatively, in the car, drive with the windows closed and the heater on. Start with five minutes and build up to fifteen minutes.

Numbness/Tingling

Hyperventilating	See previous instructions.
Putting pressure to upper arm	Raise one arm at the elbow. With your other hand apply pressure to your upper arm so the circulation is restricted. Do this for one minute; build up to two if you feel only weak sensations.
Pressing upper arm against torso	With one arm hanging loosely at your side, grasp your upper arm with the opposite hand. Grip the upper arm tightly, and press and turn it firmly against your torso. Do this for one minute; build up to two if you feel only weak sensations.

Feeling Dissociated/Detached/Unreal/Spacy

Hyperventilating	See previous instructions.
Staring at your mirror image	Stare at one spot on yourself *without deviating your gaze* at all. Do this for two minutes, then build up to three minutes.
Staring at a page full of dots or at a checkered surface	Stare intensely. Blink as little as possible. Do so for two minutes, then build up to three minutes

Feeling Weird/Confused/Disoriented

Listening to strange sounds	Find music you feel is weird or eerie (such as the music track from a haunted house movie). Or make your own recording of strange sounds or unusual music. Sit quietly and listen to the sounds. Allow yourself to experience any strange feelings that arise. Listen for at least fifteen minutes or until you feel the sensation you are trying to provoke. If you have more than one recording, start with the one that is least anxiety-provoking and work up to the more difficult ones.
Watching a strange movie	Watch a movie, videotape, or DVD you find weird or eerie. Follow the procedure for listening to strange sounds.

Creating a Migraine Aura: Spots in the Eyes, Detached Sensations

Squinting and staring	Hold your eyelids shut tightly for thirty seconds. Then open them. Stare straight ahead. Blink as little as possible. Do this exercise for thirty seconds, then for forty-five seconds. If you do not get sensations, you can build up to one or two minutes.
Staring at a page full of dots or at a checkered surface	See previous instructions.

Nausea

Eating spicy/oily foods	Eat spicy or oily foods. Pay attention to any sensations you feel. Sit quietly and focus on the sensations.
Smelling noxious odors	Find something that smells bad (for example, a rotten egg) and pass it under your nose, inhaling as you do. Focus on the sensations it creates.

Urge to Defecate

Delaying defecation	Eat a full meal. When you feel the urge to defecate, try to delay using the rest room for at least a few minutes. As you repeat this exercise, try to increase the amount of time you delay up to half an hour if you can.
Taking a laxative	Take a modest amount of an over-the-counter laxative. Follow the manufacturer's instructions. This should improve your chances of experiencing the urge to defecate. Try to experience the sensation and delay going to the rest room as instructed in the previous exercise.

Urge to Urinate

Delaying urination	Drink lots of water. When you feel the urge to urinate, try to delay using the rest room for a few minutes. As you repeat this exercise, try to increase the amount of time you delay up to half an hour if you can.

Feelings of Sadness

Watching a sad movie   Select a movie, videotape, or DVD that makes you sad. Watch the sad parts of the movie for at least fifteen minutes or until you feel sad feelings. Then sit quietly and allow yourself to experience the feelings without avoidance or distraction. There is no specific time limit, but you may need up to half an hour or more.

Listening to music   Select a recording of music that makes you sad. Sit quietly and listen to the music following the procedure previously described (see the previous exercise).

Recalling a sad event   Select a sad event from your past and focus your attention on the memory of that event, without avoidance or distraction. Follow the procedure previously described (see the "watching a sad movie" exercise).

Feelings of Anger

Watching an angry movie   Select a movie, videotape, or DVD that makes you feel angry. Watch the parts of the movie that make you feel angry for at least fifteen minutes or until you feel anger. Follow the procedure previously described (see the "watching a sad movie" exercise).

Recalling an angry event   Select an event from your past that made you angry. Sit quietly and try to recall the event. Focus your attention on it. Follow the procedure previously described (see the "watching a sad movie" exercise).

Any Feared Sensation

Focusing on a sensation   Focus your attention on the part of your body that is relevant to the sensation you want to create. For example, if you are trying to provoke light-headed feelings, focus your attention on the sensations in your head. Close your eyes to reduce distraction and to help you stay focused. Try to imagine feeling the sensation. You can even add mental suggestions (such as "I feel light-headed") to help

	strengthen the sensation. Repeat the mental suggestion and keep focusing on the relevant area of your body for at least fifteen minutes or until you feel the sensation emerge.
Imagining your feared catastrophe	Sit quietly and try to imagine your feared catastrophe is actually happening. In your mind, place yourself in the middle of the catastrophe you fear (you've fainted and everyone is laughing at you, you've had a heart attack and the ambulance is rushing you to the ER, and so on). Try to imagine what it would really be like. Hold the image of this catastrophe in your mind for at least fifteen minutes or until you feel the sensation you are trying to provoke.

Feared Sensations You Need to Target:

_____

_____

_____

_____

_____

_____

_____

_____

_____

_____

_____

_____

_____

Specific Interoceptive Exercises You Need to Work On:

_____

_____

_____

_____

_____

_____

_____

_____

_____

_____

_____

_____

_____

How to Use Worksheet 4

Use worksheet 4 to record your exposures. Try to do so systematically. The absolute ideal is to work on the relevant exercises *daily*. Doing them once in a while won't work. *Do not proceed to in vivo exposures in chapter 11 until you have overcome all your feared sensations, achieving an anxiety level of maximum 1 on each, preferably 0.* Do the exercises *alone*. If you are too fearful, do them once or twice with someone else present; then try them alone.

After having tried out an exercise once or twice and having recorded the experience, make a plan to continue with that exercise and add other relevant ones. You can work on several exercises on any given day. Remember, many take only a couple of minutes to do. If you only do one exercise daily, it may take you a long time to get through your exercises. Keep up the pace!

Remember:

1. Before you start, write down the date, the exercise you are going to do, where you will do it, and for how long.

2. During the exercise, allow yourself to fully feel the sensations. Pay attention to them. Do not use distraction.

3. Take a minute afterward to stay with the experience. Pay attention to any thoughts and feelings.

4. Afterward, write down the sensation intensity and anxiety level on the worksheet.

5. If you feel any residual anxiety, challenge it using worksheet 3 from chapter 9: Which exact sensations prompted your fear? State your catastrophic fear—the exact bad thing that you thought would happen. What was your evidence? Then refute the evidence and give alternatives. If your fear is social threat (and you truly were rejected), can you live with that?

In order to overcome agoraphobia, you must overcome the fear of sensations that make you anxious, those internal danger signals that haunt you. If you find yourself avoiding them or if you tell yourself you don't need to do these exercises, we strongly recommend you stop working with this book at this time. Or, if you have a close friend or relative who can help you through this phase, enlist his or her help! Of course, eventually you will need to do the exercises alone, but anything that helps you get started is worth trying. You can also reread the book from the beginning, for inspiration. If you remain stuck, seek out a psychotherapist with experience in the cognitive behavioral treatment of agoraphobia. We say this because you will *not* get much benefit from this program if you do it halfway.

If you *have* been able to perform the exercises successfully and have completed your work with interoceptive exposure, it is time to move on to chapter 11. *Do not move on to the next chapter unless you have completed this work.*

Worksheet 4:
Your Daily Interoceptive Exposure Log

Sensations you are provoking: _____

_____

_____

Sensation Intensity = Highest level of sensation intensity during exercise (0=lowest to 10=highest)

Anxiety Level = Highest level of anxiety/fear during exercise (0=lowest to 10=highest)

Day of Week/ Date	Name of exercise and where you are doing it	Length of Time	Sensation Intensity (0–10)	Anxiety Level (0–10)

11

Step 5. Overcoming Your Fear of Internal Sensations in the Presence of External Danger Signals

Where We're Going

Having made it to this point, you've mastered your fear of internal sensations, at least in places you perceive as safe. It's now time to deal with these sensations in the presence of external danger signals. But not so fast! Take a moment to appreciate what you've accomplished before moving on. In this chapter, we will help you develop a fear hierarchy that will guide much of the work that remains. You will confront and master the situations you fear at your own pace. As you proceed, we'll continue to encourage you to let go of counterproductive safety devices. And we will ask you to intentionally create previously feared sensations whenever possible and practical as you face each situation.

Now that you're less afraid of internal danger signals, it's time to conquer your external danger signals, or feared situations. This step involves what may be the hardest part of your recovery work: overcoming your fear of the situations that make you anxious. This step is particularly challenging because it will also involve experiencing internal sensations.

Like the previous step, step 5 will require a substantial amount of your energy and time. Research has clearly shown that the amount of exposure clients do on their own is an important predictor of successful treatment (Barlow 1988). It accounts for the largest part of the benefit received from therapy. Both the total amount of time spent practicing and the total amount of time away from "safety" (away from home or safe situations) are important. Those who practice more often and longer achieve the highest overall functioning. So it's important to practice!

How Does Exposure to External Situations Work?

When you expose yourself repeatedly to a feared situation, your physiological arousal or reaction diminishes, and little by little your psychological experience of fear diminishes as well. Put another way, you eventually learn at an emotional level that there is nothing to fear. To learn this, you must spend a great deal of time in feared situations. That is why we ask you to devote as much time as possible to your in vivo exposure work.

This does not mean you have to take on more than you can handle. Progress at your own pace. Impatience sometimes leads people to attempt difficult tasks before they have mastered easier ones. Recall that your interoceptive exposures began with easier steps. You worked yourself up to harder steps as you were able to handle them. This approach is called *graduated exposure,* taking things a step at a time. Apply this same principle to your work with external situations. Worksheet 5: Your Situational Fear Hierarchy will provide the structure for you to pace yourself.

Creating Your Situational Fear Hierarchy

A situational fear hierarchy helps you sort feared external situations into categories according to the level of anxiety they generate. You've already done the preliminary work necessary to develop your hierarchy. In chapter 3, you checked off external situations that are danger signals for you. Worksheet 2: Your Goals and Objectives that you completed in chapter 7 should also be helpful. Use these two sources of information to identify general types of situations that currently provoke anxiety. Then convert these general situations into some specific tasks. Let's say one item from your list of objectives is to "be able to eat comfortably in restaurants." This objective can be converted into tasks for your hierarchy, such as "eat lunch with my family at McDonald's," "eat lunch at Denny's with a coworker," and "eat dinner at Chez Louis with a new client."

Once you have a list of these tasks, the next step is to assign each task to one of three levels of difficulty: low-challenge, medium-challenge, and high-challenge (see worksheet 5). Low-challenge items are situations you feel would provoke an anxiety level between 1 and 3 on the 0–10 anxiety level scale (we used this same scale to rate your anxiety during your interoceptive exposures). The rating should reflect the level of anxiety you think would be provoked if you entered that situation today. Medium-challenge items are those that would provoke levels between 4 and 6, and high-challenge items are situations that would provoke levels of 7 to 10. Hence, if eating at Chez Louis with a new client would provoke an anxiety level of 8, you'd assign it to the high-challenge category. As you develop items, write them down under the appropriate category on worksheet 5. Use more than one copy of the worksheet if necessary.

Rating your anxiety is not an exact science. We realize you may not always be sure about the anxiety level you would experience. Furthermore, the comfort you feel in a situation can be influenced by many variables (how many people are there, who is there, how easy it is to escape, the weather, or how you are feeling before you go). Thus, the category to which you assign a situation may depend on certain variables. You can use these variables to generate three different levels of anxiety for similar situations, one for each level on the hierarchy. For example, take the objective, "be able to eat comfortably in restaurants." If your coworker is a close friend of yours and you only had to grab a quick bite at Denny's, you might see it as a low-challenge item. Eating with a coworker who is an acquaintance might be a medium-challenge item, and eating with a coworker you hardly know when the place is crowded might be a high-challenge item. As you can see, several variables can influence the level of anxiety provoked by a particular situation. By modifying these variables, you can identify a variety of tasks for each level of your fear hierarchy.

Before you complete the worksheet it may be helpful to look at some examples of situational fear hierarchies developed by others. Let's look at what Paul and Susie came up with. Go back to Paul's second goal, which was to accept temporary confinements without catastrophizing (see chapter 7). His objectives included attending all meetings at work, going to restaurants and other social events where he did not know people well, and accepting a jury duty summons. He prepared the following exposure hierarchy list.

Paul's Exposure Hierarchy

Low-Challenge Exposures: Anxiety Level 1–3

- Attend mandatory meetings at work while sitting near the door.

- Sit near the exit when eating in a very informal restaurant.

Medium-Challenge Exposures: Anxiety Level 4–6

- Attend all meetings at work, including optional ones, sitting farther into the room.

- Go to a restaurant with some people I don't know, sitting at an end of the table.

- Sit in the middle row in a crowded cinema.

High-Challenge Exposures: Anxiety Level 7–10

- Accept a jury duty summons.

- Sit at a meeting far from the exit and speak up, making a point or presenting an idea or other information.

- Go to a restaurant with people I do not know well, sitting far inside, so it would be cumbersome to get out.

- Take the initiative to propose and plan a family birthday party, where people I don't know well will attend. Sit in a seat with no quick exit.

Susie's Exposure Hierarchy

Low-Challenge Exposures: Anxiety Level 1–3

- Drive in heavy traffic not too far from home.

- Take a half-hour-long walk (walking fifteen minutes away from home).

- Take a short bus trip.

- Drive in unfamiliar areas.

Medium-Challenge Exposures: Anxiety Level 4–6

- Be a passenger in a car with other people for up to an hour.

- Take a one-hour-long walk (walking thirty minutes away from home).

- Go to a mall and look around for a while.

- Go to a cinema with people other than my husband.

- Take a short subway trip.

High-Challenge Exposures: Anxiety Level 7–10

- Take a longer trip on bus, subway.

- Go to restaurant, fundraiser or fair with others (without husband).

- Drive one hour away from home and back.

- Drive over bridges and freeways in heavy traffic farther from home.

- Be a passenger in a car with other people far from home.

- Go to a mall and plan to be there for at least two hours.

- Drive alone for about one hour away from home, then purposefully seek out unfamiliar areas.

- Fly in an airplane.

As you can see from Paul's and Susie's examples, time and distance are specified. For you, it may make a big difference if you drive two exits on the freeway, or ten, or if you drive on the freeway for fifteen minutes or one hour. In a department store, it may make a difference how far you are from the exit, if you are on upper floors, and how long you spend there. You can also specify where you will sit (in meetings, restaurants, cinemas): close to the aisle, close to the exit, or in the middle where it is harder to get out. You will be able to work on one or more hierarchies at a time, if you choose, but always starting with the low-challenge exposures, of course.

Complete worksheet 5 before continuing. It is not a problem if you misjudge the level of anxiety provoked by a certain situation. People often discover that particular situations generate more or less anxiety than they anticipated. When this happens, you can simply reassign the item to the appropriate category. You'll probably be modifying your hierarchy several times along the way. If you are taken by surprise, just do your best.

You may want to refer to appendix E for more information on how to face specific agoraphobic situations. There, you'll find the most commonly feared situations and ways to break them down into segments to practice on. You will be the best judge of what constitutes low-, medium-, and high-challenge exposures for you.

Worksheet 5: Your Situational Fear Hierarchy

Low-Challenge Exposures (Anxiety Levels 1–3):

_____

_____

_____

_____

_____

_____

_____

Medium-Challenge Exposures (Anxiety Levels 4–6):

_____

_____

_____

_____

_____

_____

_____

High-Challenge Exposures (Anxiety Levels 7–10):

_____

_____

_____

_____

_____

_____

_____

Planning Your Exposures

As you plan your exposures, there are a few things to consider. Following these recommendations could be crucial to your success.

Weekly Amount of Time

You need to devote time to exposures. We advise six to seven hours a week of *voluntary* exposure time spread over at least three to four days a week. You may get better eventually without devoting this much time, but it will take you longer. By voluntary time, we mean the time you reserve for exposures that is *not* a part of your normal routine. You need to devote this extra time to exposures. In order to have sufficient time, most people have to give something else up for a while (such as giving up overtime work or volunteer work, or delaying that remodeling project). If you fear walking or driving alone anywhere, you may need to do exposures *daily*. Your progress will otherwise be much too slow, and you may be inclined to give up.

When and How to Plan

Plan the days of the week and the times of day when you will do the exposures. If driving is involved, plan where, how far, and under what conditions (in light or heavy traffic, during daylight or dark, etc.). If taking elevators is involved, plan on which one to use. If you are going to the mall, decide which one to go to, for how long, and what you will do once you are there. *Then follow your plan as closely as possible.*

You may feel all this planning is too regimented. Some of our past clients felt the same way initially, yet they learned this was the best way to complete exposures. As we have seen again and again, people who approach their exposures in a more organized way are the most successful. Planning allows you to anticipate and work around obstacles. Committing to a specific time and place makes it a little more difficult to procrastinate. Those who don't plan tend to do exposures when they get a free moment. Guess what happens to them?

Length of Exposures

Ideally you will stay in a situation until your anxiety decreases, which can take from forty-five to ninety minutes or more. In some cases, it occurs more quickly than that. If you leave when the anxiety is at its peak (if you escape from the situation because you cannot stand the anxiety any more), your fear will be reinforced. This can be mitigated to a large extent if you *return quickly to the situation and try it again.* With exposures that last a short time, such as elevator or escalator rides, repeat the exposure several times in a row. Repeat the exposure also if it involves driving short distances, such as taking short freeway rides or driving the length of a bridge. You can repeat the experience again and again until your anxiety decreases.

Things You Shouldn't Do

Don't do your exposures with safety signals or safety behaviors! If you need to use one, for example, a companion as you drive across a bridge the first time, do so only once or twice and then do it without assistance. As long as you use safety devices, your exposure will be only partially effective. If you're not yet prepared to give up a safety-seeking strategy, try to phase it out as soon as you can. If you cannot phase it out, you are probably trying to do something that is too hard. It is preferable to do easier exposures without safety devices than to attempt tasks further up the fear hierarchy while engaging in secondary avoidance. You should try to establish good habits early in the process. Be patient. You'll eventually succeed with the harder tasks.

Your hierarchy of exposures can also include plans to eliminate safety devices. We will give you an example. Even though taking tranquilizers is contrary to the work in this program, we understand some people feel they need them. Carrying tranquilizers wherever you go constitutes a very powerful safety signal. This is the case *even if you never take them.* Here's how you can modify tranquilizer use to fit the hierarchy. Let's say, in your hierarchy, going grocery shopping while on a tranquilizer provokes an anxiety level of 2. You can put that situation in the low-challenge category. A medium challenge would be going to the grocery store with the tranquilizer in your pocket (but without having taken the pill). And going to the grocery store without the tranquilizer at all might be on your high-challenge list. Assign yourself each of these tasks and then complete them as you move up the fear hierarchy.

Things You Should Do

As you do your exposures, be sure to use worksheet 3. In combination with your exposures, challenging your felt beliefs with worksheet 3 can help. This worksheet is also useful in dealing with *anticipatory anxiety,* the anxiety you feel when you anticipate approaching a situation you fear. Also, you can use any of the coping skills you learned in chapter 8 (as long as you're not using them to avoid the symptom attack):

- diaphragmatic breathing

- managing the urge to escape

- objectively describing your anxiety sensations; staying in the here and now

- planning on how to cope with anxiety and panic

- developing corrective coping statements

How to Handle All-or-Nothing Thinking

If an exposure is too hard, always try to do *something*. You don't always have to do everything you set out to do. *Some* exposure is better than no exposure. Success is measured by what you do *despite how you feel* not just by what you do. You will inevitably feel anxious at first. Feeling anxious, even panicky, is not a sign of failure.

If you end up leaving an exposure situation early, before your anxiety has come down, it is not the end of the world. You can try it again the next day. Eventually you must be able to stay in the situation, but that doesn't have to be today. The good news is that as you keep doing the exposures, your anxiety and fear will diminish and your self-confidence will grow.

Self-Recognition and Self-Reward

Make sure you recognize your effort. This is hard work. You deserve some recognition. Reward yourself in different ways. At the very least, commend yourself for a job well done. Give yourself something tangible (ice cream, a back rub, or dinner and a movie) when you accomplish one of your objectives. Some people treat themselves to something nice after every exposure.

What to Do Afterward

Be sure to process your exposures after you're done. Briefly review what happened and what did not happen during the exposure. Right after completing the exposure, ask yourself three questions:

- What did your felt belief (your fear) predict would happen?

- What did your logical belief predict would happen?

- What actually occurred?

You will be able to determine which prediction was a more accurate description of what actually occurred. If no actual catastrophe occurred in spite of your anxiety, you successfully completed yet another task that proved your catastrophic prediction wrong. When you take time to process (to make a mental note of) your exposures formally, your learning will be more profound.

Carrying Out Your Situational Exposures

It's now time to begin your in vivo exposure work. Review the low-challenge items on your situational fear hierarchy in worksheet 5 and select the item or items you'll be working on first. Select those that seem the least difficult. Once you have selected them, develop your plan for the week. You'll record your experiences with external situations, just as you did with your interoceptive exposure work. You'll use worksheet 6 to keep a weekly log.

Try to follow your plan as closely as you can. Worksheets 5 and 6 will help you keep track of your progress. At any point that you feel an item from your hierarchy no longer makes you anxious, place a check next to it on worksheet 5. Some people like to keep a copy of worksheet 5 in a place where they can find it easily to check off tasks one by one. It's rewarding to begin eliminating items that used to represent restrictions in your life.

Right before you leave to do an exposure, take a minute to practice your coping strategies. If you're feeling reluctant and considering putting off an exposure, it may be helpful to complete worksheet 3. You can challenge your catastrophic fears to help you gain the proper perspective and resist the temptation to avoid exposures. If you're still tempted to put off the exposure, modify the task so it feels a little less threatening. Any step forward is better than no step at all.

During the exposure, remember to use helpful coping skills. Do everything you can to avoid safety-seeking strategies. If your anxiety level rises, the exposure is working. Allow yourself to feel the anxiety and stay with the exposure until your anxiety goes down some. Anxiety is uncomfortable, but it will not harm you. Ultimately, the only way to be free is by preparing yourself for and accepting anxiety and the sensations related to your symptom attack. You must even be prepared for a full-blown symptom attack.

Rating Your Anxiety

As you log your exposures on worksheet 6, you'll record two anxiety levels, using the same 0 to 10 scale that you used to rate your anxiety during your interoceptive exposures. This time, however, you'll be monitoring *peak* anxiety and *end* anxiety. Peak anxiety is the highest level your anxiety rose to during the entire exposure. End anxiety is the level of anxiety you experienced at the end of the exposure, right before leaving but while you were still in the situation. For each exposure, write your peak and end anxiety levels in the appropriate spaces on the worksheet.

Try to stay in the situation (or keep repeating the situation) until your anxiety comes down naturally (without the aid of safety devices or avoidance). Typically, we recommend waiting until there is at least a 50 percent drop from your peak anxiety before you stop the exposure or move on to another one. In other words, if your peak anxiety is an 8, try to maintain the exposure until your anxiety has dropped to 4 or lower. Therefore, your end anxiety level should be one-half or less of your peak anxiety level. Fifty percent is a good guideline. The lower you allow your anxiety to drop, though, the better.

How to Use Worksheet 6

At the beginning of the week, make your plan for the following week and write it down at the top of worksheet 6. Your plan should include all the details of the exposures you'll be doing that week. From worksheet 5, select the items you'll work on and write out where and when you'll do them.

At the end of each exposure exercise, write down the date and what you actually did for that exposure. Include any important parameters such as distance, use of a coach, and how long the exposure lasted. Start with a few in vivo exposures and record them under "external situation."

Record your anxiety levels as well, both peak and end levels. After your exposure is over, be sure to take a moment to process it. And don't forget to reward yourself for a job well done.

At first you'll be keeping a record of external exposures only, but, after a short amount of time, we will ask you to increase the intensity of the situations by adding some interoceptive exercises that you've already practiced.

We want you to do this because as soon as you're even somewhat comfortable in a situation, you will need to bring on the previously feared sensations. Even though you've intentionally provoked and successfully dealt with these sensations at home or in other relatively comfortable situations, your fear of these sensations has not been adequately tested in the presence of external danger signals. Recovery from agoraphobia requires the ability to deal with internal and external danger signals together. You gain this ability by repeatedly inviting and experiencing the internal sensations without avoidance while remaining in the feared situation.

As you continue to plan your exposures, go back to worksheet 4 from chapter 10. Looking at your daily interoceptive exposure log, think of which exercises you can apply to in vivo exposures. If a particular exercise in not practical to do outside of the home (like watching a VCR), consider doing the exercise right before you enter the situation you're using for exposure. A number of the exercises can be done in a parked car right before going to a restaurant, the mall, or the cinema, or on a drive. We would not recommend that you hyperventilate while standing in line, but you could hold your breath unnoticeably for, let's say, twenty to twenty-five seconds. You could also stand discreetly in a line with a cocktail straw in your mouth and breathe through it. It really helps to be creative here. If you can think of any other way of creating the relevant sensations, do so.

Often, you won't have to do anything to arouse your feared sensations while in an anxiety-provoking situation. The very sensation you fear may occur naturally without having to create it intentionally. If this happens, do not shy away from the sensation or think that this experience constitutes adequate interoceptive exposure. Instead, try to focus on the sensation and make it worse, on purpose. We know this can be very difficult to do, especially in the presence of external danger signals. The spontaneous eruption of sensations can give them greater credibility as danger signals than those you provoke on purpose. But, don't shy away from these sensations. The greatest reductions in agoraphobic fear can come from successfully exposing yourself to these experiences. Devoting your mental and behavioral efforts to intensifying a sensation is one sure way to eliminate avoidant coping. And eliminating avoidant coping is the key to recovery.

Sample Worksheets

To help familiarize you with worksheet 6, let's look at Paul's and Susie's logs. You'll notice how both of them introduce the interoceptive exercises soon after they have done in vivo exposures a few times.

Worksheet 6:
Paul's Weekly Situational Exposure Log

Exposures planned for the week starting ___6-16-03___ :

Subway to work (no safety devices). Baptism on Sunday. Many people will attend I
don't know. At work meeting sitting far from door. Go with my wife to a movie
and sit in middle of the row. On weekend take a longer subway trip. Straw
breathing, hyperventilation.

Exposures Accomplished: **Anxiety**
                                                          Level (0-10)

Day of Week/ Date	External Situation (Add distance/time)	Interoceptive Exercise (Done during or right before)	Peak	End
Mon 6-16	*Subway to work without safety devices, 45 min x2. Work meeting sitting far from door, 1 hr.*		6 4	3 3
Tues 6-17	*Subway, as above, 40 and 45 min.*		6	3
Wed 6-18	*Subway, as above, 45 min x2.*	*Straw breathing while on subway platform*	7	4
Thur 6-19	*Subway, as above, 40 and 50 min.*	*As above*	6	3
Fri 6-20	*Subway, as above, 40 min x2. Movie with wife, sitting inside the row, 2 hrs.*	*As above*	4 2	2 1
Sat 6-21	*Subway, long trip back and forth in different direction than work, 2 hrs.*	*As above*	5	1
Sun 6-22	*Baptism and afterward family gathering, sit far from exit, 3 hrs.*	*Hyperventilation in car right before entering*	6	3

Did you achieve your plan for the week? __X__ Yes _____ No
(If not entirely, are there any modifications you need to make to improve
the success of next week's plan?)

Worksheet 6:
Susie's Weekly Situational Exposure Log

Exposures planned for the week starting <u> 8-4-03 </u> :

Walk 5 days a week. Short bus trip. Mall for 1 hr. Drive in unfamiliar area, not close
to home for 15 min. Take a short subway trip and have lunch with friends. On the
weekend drive 1 hr away from home, very low traffic. Imagine or read about being
in an insane asylum.

Exposures Accomplished: **Anxiety Level (0–10)**

Day of Week/ Date	External Situation (Add distance/time)	Interoceptive Exercise (Done during or right before)	Peak	End
Mon 7-14	*Walk, 1 hr.*		*7*	*4*
Tues 7-15	*Walk, 50 min.* *Short bus trip, back & forth, 45 min.*		*6* *7*	*3* *4*
Wed 7-16	*Walk, 45 min.* *Drive in unfamiliar area, 15 min.*		*4* *6*	*2* *3*
Thur 7-17	*Walk, 1 hr.* *Go to a mall, 1hr.*	*Hyperventilate just before walk. Tightly close and open eyes in car*	*6* *5*	*1* *3*
Fri 7-18	*Walk, 1 hr.*	*Hyperventilate right before*	*4*	*2*
Sat 7-19	*Short subway trip and lunch with friends, 2.5 hrs.*		*6*	*4*
Sun 7-20	*Drive 1 hr away from home, very low traffic, 2 hrs.*	*Tightly close and open eyes in car. Hyperventilate in car while parked.*	*4*	*2*

Did you achieve your plan for the week? <u> X </u> Yes <u>   </u> No
(If not entirely, are there any modifications you need to make to improve
the success of next week's plan?)

Worksheet 6: Your Weekly Situational Exposure Log

Exposures planned for the week starting _____ :

_____

_____

_____

Exposures Accomplished: **Anxiety Level (0–10)**

Day of Week/ Date	External Situation (Add distance/time)	Interoceptive Exercise (Done during or right before)	Peak	End
Mon				
Tues				
Wed				
Thur				
Fri				
Sat				
Sun				

Did you achieve your plan for the week? _____ Yes _____ No
(If not entirely, are there any modifications you need to make to improve the success of next week's plan?)

Working Your Way up the Hierarchy

You can work on more than one feared situation at a time if you choose, but be sure to complete all the low-challenge tasks, and do them correctly, before moving to the next level of the hierarchy. That means exposing yourself to all the situations listed in the low-challenge category and gaining the confidence that you can handle those situations in the presence of internal danger signals. Only then, begin selecting items from the medium-challenge level of your hierarchy. Follow the same process through the medium-challenge items before you begin working on the high-challenge items.

Try to pace yourself. Of course you want to progress at a reasonable pace, but be careful not to rush it. The decision to move to another item on your hierarchy should be made when you have mastered the previous levels, not because you are impatient or have unrealistic expectations. If you are in a hurry, spend more time each week doing exposures, but do not skip any steps. For instance, do not skip doing interoceptive exercises in or near external danger signals. If you skip bringing on sensations, you won't progress very far.

When you have completed all of the items on your situational fear hierarchy, you are almost done working on your agoraphobia. There are just a few more things to do to make sure that your recovery is as complete as possible and that you will be able to retain your progress over time. These are the topics covered in the remaining sections of this book.

How Do You Know You Are Progressing?

This is a good time to assess if you have done all the steps described in this book. Ask yourself if you still fear the symptom attack with its accompanying sensations. It is also a time to seriously and honestly ask yourself if you have done all exposures without the use of safety signals and safety behaviors. If not, we strongly suggest that you go back and do your exposures without these safety devices and record them on worksheet 6.

You may have done many exposures and realized how your gains sometimes generalize to other situations. However, your confidence in one place will usually not spread to all situations, for each situation is to some extent unique. That is why it's important to expose yourself to as many danger signals as possible.

If there is one way of knowing you're progressing, it is that you keep moving forward. Unless and until you have overcome *all* avoidances, a standstill indicates possible trouble. An example may illustrate this best. Assume you are now able to do many things you were not doing before, including driving alone on a freeway to another town one and a half hours away. This is a good distance, and you think you don't really need or want to drive alone farther away. If you look deep within yourself, however, you may realize that if you went farther from home, something could happen, a symptom attack. The problem with having a set boundary is that you're always vulnerable when you're near it. Fear creeps back in. Hence, if you pose limits based on your comfort level, you remain at risk for your agoraphobia to return.

Summing Up

How long will this work to overcome your agoraphobia take? It is hard for us to tell you. We work with our clients from eight to twenty weeks. Some take even longer. You are working on your own. How fast you'll proceed depends on the extent of your agoraphobia, your willingness to experience temporary anxiety, and your commitment of time to doing the exposures. We'd say the last two of these three factors are the most crucial ones. We know people can do well; we have seen it in our work. Periodically, we hear of people who were very limited with their agoraphobia for some time, but then got themselves out and doing things again. Many improved remarkably even without the help of a formal program like the one outlined in this book. Is there hope? Yes, we believe there is! The important thing is to take time to do your exposures consistently and regularly, week after week, and to allow yourself to feel and tolerate anxiety and all the sensations you fear along the way. Remember, anxiety won't kill you! You become a stronger person on the other side of anxiety.

When you're ready, move on to part 3, which will help you maintain and solidify your goals.

PART 3

Evaluating and Continuing Your Progress

In part 3, you'll learn how to maintain the gains you've made. After all the work you've done, we want you to hold on to your hard-earned success. However, if you get stuck or have not progressed to the extent you had hoped, don't despair. Part 3 has something for you as well. We'll share some possible reasons why you have struggled and tell you about additional resources that might help you progress further.

12

Maintaining Your Gains

Where We're Going

Now it is time to take stock of your progress and determine what you need to do next. Hopefully, you've made good progress. If so, this chapter will help you continue and even improve upon what you have achieved. We will talk about maintenance exposures and how they can reduce your vulnerability to setbacks. If you've experienced a setback, don't worry. We also discuss how to keep temporary setbacks from developing into a prolonged relapse.

By the time you get to this chapter, you have done a great deal of work. You may be tempted to sit back and enjoy the benefits of all the effort and time you have devoted to recovery. But don't rest on your laurels too soon. The tendency to avoid is very strong and can be reignited under certain circumstances. Fortunately, there are ways to manage this problem.

Maintenance Exposures

The best way to avoid losing what you've gained is to continue exposing yourself to the things you used to fear, using a maintenance exposure plan. For some people, this may simply mean doing the things they would normally do. Once the weight of the agoraphobia has lifted and the old danger signals are no longer avoided, normal daily activity often provides a sufficient amount of exposure to maintain progress. For example, if restaurants used to be one of your external danger signals and you now eat out regularly, no extra exposure may be necessary. If, however, your normal routine does not provide enough regular exposure to avert relapse, you will need to plan periodic maintenance exposures. So, if you used to be anxious in restaurants and you do not routinely eat out, you should plan to eat out periodically. These maintenance exposures help you keep and expand the progress you've made.

Sometimes you have to go out of your way to arrange maintenance exposures, setting up activities that are not a part of your normal routine. If you have not done something for a long time, check it out. See if you can still do it. We are creatures of habit and it is easy to fall into old patterns. For example, if you are a married woman and your husband likes to drive, especially on trips out of town, make sure you drive some of the time as well, instead of just being a passenger. If your husband resists, have a heart-to-heart talk and come to some compromise acceptable to both of you. If your spouse cares, he should understand how crucial it is that you continue your exposures.

Below you can write down those areas you want to keep tabs on. These can be either reminders of what you want to pay attention to, a record of exposures that are not part of your routine and you don't want to forget, or particularly challenging exposures, be it flying, going to a high place to look out from, or being at a party where you hardly know anyone. Use this list as a reminder to keep looking for opportunities to do exposures, and going out of your way to do them. Once you seek out and expose yourself to those situations, you can record them on worksheet 7. We made this worksheet really simple to not bog you down with too much detail after all the hard work you have done. If you need to record your anxiety levels, however, you can always use worksheet 6.

Exposures You Need to Maintain Progress

_____

_____

_____

_____

_____

_____

_____

_____

_____

_____

_____

Worksheet 7: Maintenance Exposures Log

Day of Week/Date	Continued Exposures (Add Distance/Time)

You can also go back to worksheet 2, which outlines your goals and objectives, and assess if you've accomplished all of them. Also determine if you are satisfied with your progress, and add new items if you'd like. For example, after accomplishing her original goals and objectives, Susie wanted to visit a close friend in another state, about one and a half hours away by plane. She decided to write a new goal with its objectives. She was now ready to increase her range of mobility and freedom. Do you need to set a new goal, or are you okay with the ones you set earlier? If you have a new goal and objectives, repeat the steps as you have done until now. Always strive for more freedom.

Managing Setbacks: Making Sure They're Temporary

Be prepared for setbacks! Effective management begins with the understanding that setbacks are normal. A setback is a temporary return of anxiety about having a symptom attack. This is to be expected. Improvement never goes in a straight line. If your overall movement is in a forward direction, you are progressing. Taking three steps forward and two steps backward may be discouraging, but it is not unusual during certain stages of recovery.

A full-blown symptom attack or the sensations signaling it can and will happen at one time or another. But remember, if you no longer fear the symptom attack and do not resort to avoidance, the setback is likely to be brief.

When a setback occurs, how will you respond? Hopefully, you won't conclude, "My recovery is over. I'm doomed." On the contrary, if you take what we've said to heart, you'll be prepared for this event and use the strategies you need to cope effectively. A setback, even a relapse, is an opportunity to strengthen your learning further, if you handle it right. And you may be surprised at how quickly you can turn things around. It's always easier to brush up on a language you haven't used in a while than it is to learn a language for the first time. If you succeeded before, you can beat it now a second time around, and faster! Much faster! The most important thing is to use the principles you've learned, and to not give up.

Circumstances That May Trigger Fear Anew

The following circumstances may trigger a setback:

- A symptom attack occurs unexpectedly and you were not prepared for it. It may have occurred even though things seem perfectly smooth in your life at the time.

- You experience sensations that are different from before or that occurred in a different place. These sensations are new danger signals that you have not yet challenged.

- You stop using the tools you learned before, such as challenging fearful, negative thoughts.

- You're going through a highly stressful time in your life. (Pay attention to your stress level if it starts building up. Is there something you can do to decrease your stress level or the way you handle it?)

- You're overly tired or ill and feel vulnerable.

- You were taking medications and stopped too suddenly.

If you have a return of anxiety after not having it for a long time, think of it as a wake-up call. Instead of getting obsessed with the anxiety, ask yourself why it happened *now*. Anxiety does not occur in a vacuum, isolated from the rest of your life. Most likely it happened because you either had some feelings you did not fully accept or were not dealing with something you needed to deal with. You may have to analyze things in your life very closely. Remember, when we hide things that bother us, it is likely to cause anxiety. Even if you can't figure it out, don't let avoidance take over. Follow the strategies to help you prevent setbacks from becoming a relapse.

Strategies to Help Reduce Setbacks

As we have said, the most reliable way to maintain your progress is to keep exposing yourself to danger signals. However, there are other things you can do. You can use the following strategies:

- Incorporate coping skills, discover negative automatic thoughts, and refute them using worksheet 3. You can modify the worksheet to cover situations not related to anxiety. The principle is the same.

- Develop a plan to restart regular exposures. Follow your plan.

- Engage in regular physical exercise. That means having a good workout at least three times a week. It will help you deal better with stress. Use other strategies to help you manage stress. For more information on stress management we recommend *The Relaxation and Stress Reduction Workbook* (Davis, et al. 2000).

- Be assertive: Stand up for yourself! Or take steps to solve the problem that is creating stress. The more you exert interpersonal control, the better you will feel. You will be less likely to displace a sense of lack of control from a real-life situation to an imaginary one. This means that while the challenges in dealing with people are real ones, the feared catastrophes are imaginary ones: they are not real or catastrophic. There are excellent books to help you develop assertiveness.

13

What to Do If You Get Stuck

Where We're Going

This chapter is for those of you who are dissatisfied with your level of progress. In it we suggest reasons why you may have struggled and discuss strategies and resources that might help you progress. Try not to be too discouraged. You still have options.

If you have not progressed as you had hoped, if you got stuck at some point along the way, it is important not to give up. Please don't waste time criticizing yourself or putting yourself down. That will only make you feel worse, and, more importantly, distract you from discovering the real reasons for your lack of progress and what you can do about it.

Why People Don't Get Better

From our experience, a number of issues may interfere with progress.

Perhaps it's not the right time. Look at your life right now. Are you experiencing major stress? Have you taken on too many competing responsibilities? Are you too busy to devote the time it takes to overcome your agoraphobia? If you answered "yes" to any of these questions, it may not be the best time for you to tackle your agoraphobia. You may have to wait until things get less hectic or take steps to lessen the current demands on your time and energy.

You may need to address another problem. Do you have another problem that is getting in your way? Often, people with agoraphobia have at least one other significant problem. If you are severely depressed, you may not have the energy or desire necessary to follow the steps in this book. Drinking or drug abuse can also interfere with recovery from agoraphobia. Other types of anxiety disorders can accompany agoraphobia and complicate the recovery process. If you are experiencing a problem of this magnitude, it may need attention before you can address your agoraphobia successfully.

Perhaps you did not follow all the steps adequately. We are not saying you purposefully sabotaged your recovery. There are many reasons why you may not have performed all of the steps correctly. You may have tried to rush through the steps and missed key points. You may have misunderstood some parts of the book. You may have taken shortcuts, underestimating their impact on the outcome. If you think you may not have followed all the steps properly, we suggest you do some serious soul-searching. Review this book, chapter by chapter, and answer these questions: Did you make time to work on this program? Did you read each chapter carefully in its entirety? Did you fill out all the worksheets? Did you do the exposures exactly as we suggested? Did you let go of all your safety devices? If you answered "no" to any of these questions, you may need to go through certain parts or the entire book again.

Perhaps you cannot do this on your own. The reality is that overcoming agoraphobia is simply too difficult for some people to accomplish on their own. There is no shame in needing help from others. Many of our clients have told us that they are grateful they did not have to deal with their agoraphobia by themselves. If you are unable to do this on your own, please consider getting professional assistance. We discuss this option in more detail below.

Other Resources

Help is always available, one way or another. There are many therapists throughout the nation who know how to help people with agoraphobia. There are also a few other self-help resources besides this book.

Getting Professional Help

If you cannot progress on your own, please seek professional help. There is no need for you to give up and accept a life with agoraphobia. This program is a self-help version of cognitive behavioral therapy (CBT), the most powerful treatment for agoraphobia. CBT helps people work on their thoughts, feelings, and behaviors, just as we have tried to do in this book you can use the resources discussed in the next section (Self-Help Resources) to locate a therapist familiar with CBT. Other forms of psychotherapy will not make agoraphobia go away. Medication can help people feel better, but it seldom makes phobias go away. Also, when medication is discontinued, things are likely to return to square one.

Consider combining CBT with medications only if your agoraphobia is moderate to severe or you have other conditions that require medication. If you are willing to wait for the cognitive behavior therapy to work, it is often worthwhile trying it first, without using medication. Naturally, you should discuss any medication changes with a physician who knows your condition. If you are considering medication, you may want to revisit our discussion of drug treatments in chapter 5.

Self-Help Resources

Below are some helpful resources that you might want to use. The Anxiety Disorders Association of America (ADAA) is an excellent resource. They can give you names of therapists in your area. They also have yearly conferences, open to consumers as well as professionals. If you attend, they provide a great deal of support and events specifically targeted to consumers. The ADAA is also a good resource for finding a support group in your area.

Local phobia and anxiety support groups are available in many cities and have meetings for people who struggle with phobias and anxiety. Groups are particularly helpful if they promote learning and support for doing exposures.

They are less helpful if they have become a vehicle to commiserate over how awful it is to live with phobias.

If you also suffer from obsessive-compulsive disorder, consider becoming a member of the OC Foundation. This organization is another great resource.

Freedom from Fear is a good national resource. This is the group that organizes the yearly "Anxiety disorders Screening Day," which takes place in early May.

Here are the organizations that may be able to help you, and how to contact them.

- Anxiety Disorders Association of America (ADAA)
  (301) 231-9350; www.adaa.org

- National Institute of Mental Health (NIMH)
  (800) 64 PANIC (647-2642); www.nimh.nih.gov

- OC Foundation
  (203) 315-2190; info@ocfoundation.org; www.ocfoundation.org

- Freedom from Fear
  (718) 351-1717

APPENDIX A

Why Some People Develop Panic and Phobias

In chapter 1 you read about the physiology of fear and panic. Here, we will elaborate on the difference between a fear reaction to true imminent danger, or a true alarm, and a panic attack, or false alarm. Reading about the physiology of fear, you may wonder what it has to do with panic attacks. The sympathetic nervous system is stimulated in a number of situations. Stressors besides fear can activate it. Emotional upheaval is one of the more common precipitants of the stress response. This means that the fight/flight response can be elicited rather easily. Is there an advantage to this? If you think of the importance of survival, you'll understand why it is better for your body to be more reactive than too slow. You do not want to be in the process of dying before you realize you are in danger.

A large percentage of the normal population has an occasional false alarm. This occurs particularly in high-stress situations, such as during public speaking or while taking an important test. But a number of people have *unexpected* (that is, out of the blue) false alarms, about 12 percent of the population. Most people do not develop panic disorder; only 3.5 percent of the population does. Hence, the average person with a false alarm is able to explain it away in nonthreatening terms. You may ask, "Why don't I do the same? Why did I develop phobias or panic?" Research has shown that three factors contribute to the development of anxiety disorders: a biological predisposition, psychological vulnerabilities, and a major stressor. All three factors need to line up for these conditions to develop. People who are thus predisposed—in the absence of an outside danger—are likely to turn the source of danger inward: they believe they'll have a heart attack, suffocate, go crazy, and so on.

Physical symptoms constitute the *physiological* component of panic. If you interpret the sensations in your body as indicating a disease or loss of functioning, and you expect disaster, fear results. Similarly, you may look for ways in which you are trapped and believe you cannot flee. These negative thoughts or misinterpretations of what the sensations mean represent the *cognitive,* or *mental,* component of panic. The *behavioral* component of panic, naturally, consists of behaviors, or overt acts. You may feel restless during a panic and pace back and forth, become easily irritable, and later avoid situations where you might feel trapped. Escaping from situations when you have a panic attack is common, as you know. After all, the impulse to escape is built into the fight/flight response; it is understandable that you may have the urge to flee. Because of the misinterpretation of internal danger, you may go to an emergency room repeatedly, seeking reassurance.

A Major Difference between Fear and Panic

In panic, the physical reactions are the same as those you experience during fear when you are in true danger. The difference is that there is no outlet. If you panic when you are in a traffic jam on a bridge, you do not have someone to fight and you cannot very well leave your car and flee. Yet your body has prepared itself for such action. There is now too much oxygen coming in compared to your body's need. This leads to diminished oxygen release to the tissues. As a result of less oxygen to the tissues, including the brain, you may have feelings of light-headedness, dizziness, feelings of unreality, or blurred vision. You may try to compensate by breathing harder, perhaps causing yourself discomfort and chest pain. So here is the paradox: You may feel as if you are not breathing enough air, when in fact you are *taking in more oxygen than you need!*

APPENDIX B

How Negative Automatic Thoughts Reflect Cognitive Traps

Many negative automatic thoughts reflect cognitive traps. They are called irrational thoughts (also called *cognitive distortions*) or unhelpful thoughts (also called *maladaptive thoughts*). In chapter 8, we described the two mistakes that lead people to exaggerate danger: probability errors and severity errors. In this appendix we discuss further the cognitive distortions responsible for agoraphobia. As you challenge your catastrophic fears with worksheet 3, learn to recognize which cognitive traps you are falling into and start to question them. Reflect on them and challenge them instead of taking your beliefs to be absolute truths.

Irrational or Unhelpful Thoughts

Of all the cognitive distortions a person may fall into, here are the most common ones in phobic and panic situations (Zuercher-White 1998).

Exaggerating or overestimating risk. Overestimating means to greatly exaggerate the odds of a dangerous or bad event happening. Although there is no absolute certainty in life, the probability of certain events occurring is so remote that assuming they will happen *right now* is irrational. Here are some examples of this kind of thinking:

- "If I drive on the freeway, I will get so dizzy and light-headed that I will faint and cause an accident."

- "If I am far from home and feel detached and unbearably anxious, I will go insane."

Catastrophizing. Catastrophizing is closely related to overestimating. There are two versions:

1. Not only could the bad event take place, but extreme and horrible consequences will follow. It involves imagining the worst-case scenario: "If the anxiety continues and I can't gather my thoughts, I'll lose it totally and become dysfunctional. I will not be able to hold down a job."

2. The person underestimates his or her ability to cope with the event. This involves often feeling unbearably embarrassed: "What if others see me shaking so badly that they think I'm crazy? I would feel so embarrassed that I could never face those people again.

Catastrophizing reflects the part of the severity error that has to do with social threat (embarrassment, humiliation, and emotional reactions such as, "I cannot cope with or handle if X were to happen").

Trying to have control at all costs. People with fears have an issue with two kinds of control: Wanting *control over outside events,* and wanting *full control over their emotions* at all times. Here are some examples:

- "I can't stand situations where I am not in control: stuck in traffic, waiting in a waiting room, flying, being a passenger in a car, sitting in the middle of the row in a movie theater or auditorium, sitting in a group meeting, or being at the dentist."

- "I should be able to control my emotions. Other people do."

Using emotions and sensations as evidence. We take our emotions and physical sensations as evidence of reality—that is, if something is felt, it must be true. This involves the notion that the stronger something is felt, the more it is a sign of truth. Examples of this kind of thinking include:

- "When I feel my heart beating so fast, it must mean I'm going to have a heart attack."

- "When I feel so much fear, I know that something awful will happen. Feelings don't lie."

Expecting Disaster. Disaster expectation is particularly common in chronic worriers. There are three versions of this. Versions two and three are examples of magical thinking, which is actually irrational thought. The third version is common in panic and phobias.

1. Many people think that they could not possibly cope if bad things happen *unexpectedly*. The thinking goes, "I'll expect the worst. Then, if the worst does not happen, I'll be grateful."

2. Magical thinking may be the belief that worrying about a danger somehow ensures that it will *not* happen. Few people openly admit to thinking this way, but it is very common. If you worry intensely and nothing bad happens, it reinforces the notion that the worrying helped. Some people justify this thought pattern by thinking, "God will spare me. I paid my dues worrying. He would not have let me worry for nothing."

3. Here is another form of magical thinking: After many uneventful episodes, your luck will run out and the bad event will happen. You think, "I haven't lost my bowels in public yet. I have always gotten to the bathroom on time, but the next time I may not be so lucky."

Giving up. This is another unhelpful or maladaptive way of thinking. If you have tried a few avenues and decided there is no hope, you are giving up. This has occurred for many people with agoraphobia. The task seems too big to handle. Yet if the person were to take one step at a time, as with this program, he or she may never have to feel the need to give up.

Appendix C

Factual Information about Symptom Attacks

Many people with agoraphobia are misinformed about the symptom attacks they fear. Misinformation can lead you to overestimate danger. Here we provide accurate medical and psychological information about some of the most commonly feared symptom attacks, including the causes and real-versus-imagined dangers associated with each symptom attack. Information about panic attacks is not included here since this type of symptom attack is covered thoroughly in other sections of the book.

Fainting

Fainting is a brief loss of consciousness due to inadequate amounts of oxygen in the brain. It occurs when the heart is not pumping efficiently enough at a particular moment to maintain adequate blood flow to the head. Right before fainting, a person often feels faint, an experience that can include feeling weak, nauseated, and dizzy or light-headed. The feeling is often that of simply fading away. Blurred vision or sweating may also occur.

Fainting can also be referred to as *swooning, passing out,* or *blacking out.* The medical term for fainting is *syncope.*

What Causes It?

A number of things can cause fainting, including poor blood circulation, pain, drug or alcohol use, dehydration, sleep deprivation, head injury, seizure, heart disease or stroke, very restrictive dieting, mineral deficiency (in particular potassium), some medications, and even certain body responses, like severe coughing or laughing.

Contrary to popular belief, anxiety does not typically trigger fainting. Since passing out is associated with low blood pressure and anxiety involves a rise in blood pressure, people are actually less likely to faint when they're anxious than when they're in a normal state. There is one notable exception. People with a blood-injury-injection phobia sometimes faint. They become anxious when they see blood, needles, or other things associated with injury or medical care. When confronted with the feared stimuli, they experience an initial rise in blood pressure characteristic of anxiety, followed quickly by a dramatic drop in blood pressure. This drop of blood pressure below normal levels is unique in people with this type of phobia and does not occur in any other type of anxiety or fear. The same people who might faint at the sight of a needle do not faint in connection with other types of phobias or anxiety they may experience. If you happen to have a blood-injury-injection phobia, you should know that it is a very treatable condition. Specific cognitive behavioral therapy procedures have been developed to treat it.

Is It Dangerous?

Most fainting spells are due to relatively benign triggers and are not a sign of serious illness. However, you should inform your physician of any unexplained fainting spells, just to be on the safe side. The fainting response itself is not generally dangerous. Though fainting episodes can last up to several minutes, most last no more than ten or fifteen seconds, and often even less than that. The only danger is when you are in a position (standing up) that makes you vulnerable to injury if you were to lose consciousness too rapidly. However, fainting is usually preceded by a clear warning signal (fading away), so you have time to lie down or take other precautions before passing out. The feelings of light-headedness and dizziness experienced in the context of anxiety and panic are not a sign you're about to faint.

Headache

A headache is exactly what the name implies—a pain in your head. Almost everyone has experienced a headache sometime in their life. There are three main types of headache:

1. By far, *tension headaches* are the most common. Ninety percent of all headaches are tension headaches. This type of headache involves sustained contraction of the neck and head muscles and often feels like a tight band wrapped around your head.

2. *Migraine headaches* occur when blood vessels in the scalp dilate. They affect less than 7 percent of the general population but are more likely to occur in women. Most commonly, migraines involve intense pain on one side of the head or behind the eyes. There is also a less common form of this type of headache, sometimes referred to as a *pseudomigraine.* This does not always involve severe pain but causes temporary disorientation and other sensations. Migraines are sometimes preceded by auras (visual distortions like flashes of light or zigzag lines) and usually last up to a few hours. In some cases, they can linger for days.

3. Less common are *cluster headaches,* experienced by less than 1 percent of the population. They are more likely to occur in men. Cluster headaches tend to be extremely painful, involving a severe burning or gnawing pain around one eye that can last a couple of hours. They often occur in episodes (such as daily for a month) and then go away for months or even years.

What Causes It?

Many things can cause headaches and most of them are comparatively benign. Stress, caffeine withdrawal, colds, and the flu are common contributors to headaches. Less than 5 percent of the time, a serious cause is involved. Examples of serious causes of headaches are allergies, high blood pressure, brain hemorrhage, stroke, brain tumor, meningitis, Lyme disease, tapeworm, glaucoma, an abscessed tooth, and some medications.

Is It Dangerous?

As we've already mentioned, headaches are not a sign of serious illness in the vast majority of cases. If you have any questions about the nature of your headaches, consult your physician. They are certainly unpleasant and can temporarily interfere with your ability to think and function, but those effects are typically manageable and do not last. It is useful to have strategies for coping with headaches (have pain relievers handy, find a quiet place to lie down) that you can implement when they occur. The purpose of these strategies is to manage the pain and avoid aggravating it. Headaches do not make people lose control of their mind or go insane, as some people with agoraphobia fear.

Loss of Bladder Control

Loss of bladder control refers to unwanted loss of urine from the bladder. The medical term for this is *incontinence,* also referred to as *enuresis.* Problems with bladder control are relatively common, but disproportionately affect women and the elderly. There are three types of incontinence:

1. *Stress incontinence* is when you urinate accidentally in response to strain on the bladder caused by laughing, coughing, sneezing, or exerting yourself.

2. *Urge incontinence* happens when the bladder contracts and empties whenever it is full, despite your effort to control it. The person is aware of the urge to urinate but cannot adequately control the bladder and delay urination when needed. The response can be so automatic and happen so quickly that people with urge incontinence are often unable to get to the rest room on time.

3. *Overflow incontinence* is when urine leaks from the bladder either because the person is unaware of the urge to urinate or because the bladder was not fully emptied. Men with large prostate glands may have difficulty fully emptying their bladder and thus may leak urine after they urinate. In other instances, medication or neurological disease can deaden the nerves responsible for alerting you to the need to urinate.

What Causes It?

As you probably already guessed, incontinence has a variety of causes. Some of them include neurological problems, infection, atrophic vaginitis, psychological problems such as depression, medication, excess urine (from drinking large amounts of liquids or from the effects of diabetes), restrictions in mobility (inability to get to the rest room quickly), and severe, chronic constipation. It is important to determine the cause and type of incontinence because treatments vary.

Is It Dangerous?

Like many symptoms, incontinence is sometimes a sign of serious illness. And you should always discuss any symptoms of concern with your physician. However, more often it is simply an embarrassing and disruptive nuisance. The symptom itself is not a threat to your physical well-being. It will not make you lose control of your mind or go insane. Most people would be embarrassed if they lost control of their bladder, whether they have a phobia or not, but would not negatively judge others with bladder control problems. Even if someone were to treat you negatively, it would not be a catastrophe. You might feel embarrassed, but you would survive the experience.

Loss of Bowel Control

Loss of bowel control refers to unwanted, uncontrollable leakage of stool from the anus. It is also referred to as *bowel incontinence, fecal incontinence,* and *encopresis.* Bowel control problems are more common among people over sixty-five and children, but others develop it as well.

What Causes It?

The causes of bowel control problems include chronic constipation (which can eventually lead to rebound diarrhea), severe diarrhea (which can be caused by food or lactose intolerance, bacterial infection, or viral gastroenteritis), stress or emotional disturbance, damage to nerves or muscles involved in defecation (from stroke, trauma, or tumor), aftereffects of surgery, severe hemorrhoids or rectal prolapse, decreased awareness of sensations related to bowel fullness, and chronic laxative abuse.

Is It Dangerous?

Losing control of your bowels is not dangerous. The symptom attack itself is not harmful and most episodes of fecal incontinence are not tied to a serious medical condition. However, if an episode persists for more than a week or you're experiencing other symptoms of concern (such as losing weight), be sure to discuss your condition with your physician. There are no serious psychological or social dangers involved in bowel incontinence. Losing control of your bowels can be stressful, but it cannot make you go crazy or lose control of your mind. Most people experience some disgust and embarrassment when it happens but are able to cope with the situation. People generally find the odor and sight of fecal matter unpleasant, but most do not negatively judge someone who is experiencing bowel control problems. The response is usually one of understanding and the desire to assist if needed. You *could* encounter a person who is judgmental about bowel incontinence. However, you'll find you are able to cope with this situation if it were to happen.

Vomiting

Vomiting is the forceful discharge of stomach contents through the mouth. It is distinguished from *regurgitation,* which is typically a milder response involving the return of stomach contents to the mouth. Vomiting involves the simultaneous contraction of muscles in the throat, diaphragm, and abdomen triggered by signals from the brain. The medical term for vomiting is *emesis.* Although unpleasant, vomiting serves an important purpose because it helps the body get rid of potentially harmful substances.

What Causes It?

A number of things can cause vomiting. The main job of the part of the brain that controls vomiting is to monitor your bloodstream and digestive system for toxins. Thus, the presence of harmful substances in your body is the primary trigger for vomiting. However, the brain's vomit control center interacts closely with a part of the brain that monitors your sense of smell, taste, sight, and equilibrium. That is why people sometimes vomit when seeing or smelling something disturbing or encountering a rough ride at sea. The causes of vomiting include certain gastrointestinal and abdominal disorders, some medications, nervous system disorders (motion sickness, inner ear disorders), hormonal changes (early stages of pregnancy, diabetic ketoacidosis), infections, and overconsumption of alcohol.

Is It Dangerous?

Vomiting is a natural, protective response of the body. There are a few situations (someone is unconscious or has a serious medical complication) when vomiting has some risk of causing physical harm, but vomiting is not acutely dangerous under normal circumstances. Despite what some people fear, vomiting cannot make you incapacitated or lose control of your mind. The mental distraction and discomfort that accompany this bodily response stop as soon as the act of vomiting is over. Excessive concerns about vomiting in front of other people are also unfounded. The vast majority of people respond to someone vomiting with empathy and understanding. If someone were to respond negatively, you might become temporarily upset, but you could cope.

APPENDIX D

The Physiology and Symptoms of Hyperventilation

When you breathe too much compared with what you need at the time, some of the excess oxygen gets released during exhalation. More importantly, too much carbon dioxide is expelled. Continued overbreathing forces some of the carbon dioxide, which always is in the arteries, to be exhaled as well. This results in the blood becoming more alkaline, or less acidic, and this leads quickly to some other changes, resulting in hyperventilation. Oxygen becomes more tightly bound to the hemoglobin (the hemoglobin becomes oxygen-sticky), and blood vessels constrict in the brain and other parts of the body. Both events result in less oxygen becoming available for the cells in their metabolism. While hyperventilation is in no way dangerous, it produces uncomfortable sensations. When this happens in the brain, the symptoms produced are dizziness, light-headedness, feelings of unreality, and blurred vision. Less oxygen in the extremities produces tingling sensations, numbness, and cold. Hyperventilation produces other sensations as well, including chest pain. All of these symptoms mimic closely the symptoms of a panic attack; the two conditions are often indistinguishable.

About one-third of people with panic disorder have been shown to hyperventilate chronically, and many panic attacks are associated with acute hyperventilation. Though we are unaware of any studies on this, we speculate that those who fear suffocation during a panic attack may tend to hyperventilate and make it worse by trying to breathe harder. Hyperventilation produces a paradox. When people hyperventilate, they feel as if they are not getting enough air when in fact they are breathing too much. Any attempt to breathe more exacerbates the hyperventilation. They usually do not know that they need to breathe less.

Signs of possible hyperventilation are upper chest (thoracic) breathing, breathing through the mouth rather than the nose, eighteen or more breaths per minute when relaxed (standing, lying down, sitting), frequent sighing, gasps (sudden, fast inhalations), yawning, coughing or clearing of the throat, moistening of the lips, and outwardly apparent heavy breathing.

People often imagine that hyperventilation symptoms, acute or chronic, will lead to fainting. In fact, the kidneys have a compensatory mechanism that restores the pH level and thus makes the blood more acidic again. The symptoms then subside. However, continued irregular breathing, mild exertion, or stress can make the symptoms return. Hyperventilation symptoms may come and go.

Many people, especially those in urban areas with their hectic and stressful lifestyles, get into the habit of upper chest breathing. This type of breathing can result in hyperventilation.

Ways to Stop Hyperventilation

There are four ways to stop hyperventilation. We recommend diaphragmatic breathing for most situations, but you may find some of these other methods helpful. You can try them all.

Hold your breath. In order to hold in the carbon dioxide longer, take a breath and then hold it for ten to twenty seconds, whatever feels comfortable. Then take a breath and hold it again. Do this several times in a row until your hyperventilation symptoms dissipate.

Breathe in and out of a paper bag. The reason this stops hyperventilation is that you will keep breathing in the carbon dioxide you exhaled into the bag. This has limitations. Carrying a paper bag becomes a safety signal. Also, you are not likely to breathe in and out of a paper bag while driving or attending a meeting or sitting in a classroom.

Vigorous exercise. Aerobic exercises, such as running or walking up and down stairs quickly, increase your metabolism. You will be using the extra oxygen you took in. Again, there are limitations on where and when you can do this.

Diaphragmatic breathing. This is the best way to stop hyperventilation. If you are a chronic hyperventilator, you may want to retrain yourself to breathe correctly.

Appendix E

Specific Feared Agoraphobic Situations

Different feared situations have their own unique challenges. Below are descriptions of some specific agoraphic situations, along with suggestions on how to go about exposure planning.

Driving a Car

We cannot always predict people's feared catastrophe based on the internal sensations that bother them. However, there are some combinations that are common when driving is the external danger signal.

While driving, sensations of dizziness and light-headedness are often related to the fear of fainting; feelings of numbness in the legs and arms (being paralyzed with fear) are often related to the notion that you will not be able to move the steering wheel or press on the gas or brake pedals (thereby causing an accident); a feeling of unreality is often related to the thought that you will be so distracted that you won't know what you are doing on the road. This is a good place to use worksheet 3. As you do so, look at your own or other people's past experience or logic. That is, have you actually lost consciousness while driving or not? Whatever you felt, did you actually manage to get off the road? If you did, you had control in spite of the sensations. *Always look at your behavior, not the sensations* or how you felt.

The following is frequently given as evidence of the danger of freeway driving: "But I have done dangerous things like using the brakes to slow the car way down, or speeding up." Yet think about it, the fear in these instances is really about something else, like the examples we just gave. Slowing down the car (or speeding up in order to quickly get off the bridge or to the next freeway exit) is the *attempted solution.* To clarify, ask yourself how you feel when you slow down the car. Your answer is invariably that you feel better because you feel in greater control. This tells you that it is the attempted solution.

Ask yourself, if you do not slow down the car, what is the awful thing that would happen? Unfortunately, the "solution" of slowing down, *unlike the feelings and thoughts of anxiety,* is actually dangerous. Other drivers do not expect a car in front of them to suddenly slow down for no reason. Hence, for your safety, *do not unexpectedly slow down the car,* even when you have uncomfortable sensations. Less frequent, but similarly, you might suddenly speed up the car, going much faster than the speed limit. Answer the question, if you kept at the normal speed, what is the awful thing that would happen?

Suggestions on Exposure Planning

If you don't drive alone at all because of fear, take small but frequent steps to do so. Do the exposures daily.

- Drive around the block, repeating three to four times, doing several loops.

- Add more blocks.

- Drive around your neighborhood.

- Drive to nearby small stores or the bank.

- If you initially use a coach, use the person only once or twice. Then have the coach follow you in another car once or twice, then do it alone.

- Work you way up to more difficult driving challenges, like major roads and highways. You can go small distances, but always repeat several loops.

- Keep adding greater distance or new places new as soon as possible.

For freeway driving, we suggest that you

- Use a coach if necessary, maybe once to be your passenger, then following you in another car. Then do it alone.

- If getting on the freeway is difficult, drive on a major highway first, if there is one near you. An ideal highway is a rather straight one where you can drive forty-five or fifty miles an hour.

- Drive only the distance between the on-ramp and the first off-ramp, or exit. In other words, get on the freeway and take the next exit. Ideally, choose a freeway entrance where you don't have to merge, where the same lane that you used to enter the freeway will also allow you to exit.

- Add more exits; drive on different parts of the freeway; use other freeways.

- As you keep practicing, loosen your grip on the steering wheel, use coping strategies as long as they are not avoidant.

- If you are using a coach, let the coach follow you in another car, with longer and longer stretches of roadway between the two of you.

- Eventually, change lanes, drive at different times of the day, with different amounts of traffic, in rain or shine, on good or bad days.

- Drive increasingly longer segments.

- Bridges cannot be broken up into small segments. Work on them later.

Public Transportation, Taxis, Trains, and Airplanes

In public transportation, some people tend to feel trapped, without an exit. Much of this sense of entrapment has to do with social apprehension. For some people the fear here takes place while waiting at the departing station, where you may have to sit on the bus, train, or airplane for awhile with the doors open. You may feel torn: "Do I leave, or do I stay?"

Suggestions on Exposure Planning

- Go into the airport or train station and sit for awhile. Watch planes taking off, trains departing. Imagine yourself there.

- With a coach, go to the next station.

- With a coach, travel farther by bus or train.

- Have the coach take an earlier bus or train and meet you at a specified station.

- Take public transportation alone.

- Take public transportation during a busy time of the day.

- Go alone during rush hour as far as the last station and then return.

- With flying, take a short flight first, preferably somewhere you expect to have a lot of fun. We recommend the book *Flying without Fear* (Brown 1996).

Going to Stores and Malls

Here the common fears are feeling shaky, fainting, not reaching the bathroom on time, losing control, and otherwise making a spectacle.

Suggestions on Exposure Planning

- If you are using a coach, have your coach wait for you inside the store or mall. Enter the building, spend five minutes there, and leave without purchasing anything.

- The coach can be a few steps behind you, with longer and longer distances between the two of you as you progress. Purchase something.

- The coach waits outside while you enter and stand in a short line to purchase an item. Then do this without the coach.

- If you use a cart, loosen your grip on the handle. Make sure you can be in a store without a cart as well.

- Spend increasingly more time inside, select more items to purchase, stand in longer lines. At times, look for the longest line you can find!

- Go inside the mall via different entrances and exits.

- Spend increasingly longer periods in the store or mall, up to two hours or more at one time.

Going to Movies, Theaters, and Auditoriums

If you fear being trapped, again we suggest that you practice leaving places according to a preset amount of time. This is much more practical in a cinema than at live theater or a concert. Plan in advance how long you think you can stay. It may be ten, fifteen, or thirty minutes. Excuse yourself when your time limit is up and then leave. That is, leave on purpose. Practice however many times you need to *until you no longer feel trapped.* Then practice staying for the entire event.

Suggestions on Exposure Planning

- You can do this one with a coach in the beginning, but do it alone as soon as possible.

- Go to a movie theater and choose a seat near the aisle at first.

- After a predetermined length of time, leave the movie theater and go home.

- Go to a movie theater and sit several seats from the aisle. *Plan to take a break* at a certain predetermined time (say, fifteen minutes after your arrival), go to the bathroom or out to the lobby, and return ten minutes later.

- Eventually, go to a movie theater and sit in the middle of the row.

- Go alone and remain for the *entire* movie.

- Also practice going to auditoriums, live theaters, and concerts.

Being Alone at Home

People fear being alone for various reasons. If you fear someone will break in and hurt you, this fear constitutes a specific phobia about being harmed by others and is not agoraphobia. If you fear being alone because you may have a symptom attack, then the phobia is agoraphobia. You associate the symptom attack with a feared catastrophe. Sometimes people associate being alone with dying or going insane and having no one there to rescue them.

Suggestions on Exposure Planning

- Stay home alone for ten minutes at first, then more or less as you can tolerate it.

- Stay home alone for thirty minutes and call a family member or friend according to a preset plan. (The call should be just to say "Hi" and not to spend the remainder of the time in contact "in case something bad happens.")

- Stay home alone for one hour with someone available to call but without you calling this person.

- Stay home alone for increasingly longer periods of time without having lined up a person to call.

- Stay home alone in the evening, even at night, if possible. The first one or two times you can call someone to check in, but then do it without checking in.

Social Apprehensions

Social apprehensions include the fear of being looked at, showing signs of anxiety, or being in close proximity to someone, such as a dentist or hairdresser. (A number of people feel trapped at the dentist and hairdresser.) You may fear getting up at a meeting, or from a dinner table (at a restaurant), or while sitting at the cinema, a theater, or other places because you are afraid that people will look at you. When everyone is seated, it is natural for their eyes to move to the person who is standing up, and you may fear being negatively judged. If people's eyes go to you, *it does not necessarily mean they are thinking negatively about you.* People may be momentarily annoyed if you block their view while getting up from the middle of the row in a movie or a similar situation, but their annoyance or irritation is very short-lived.

Suggestions on Exposure Planning

- If you have to give a speech in a meeting, say you are nervous. (You can do this in many, albeit not all, public-speaking situations.)

- If you fear looking crazy, practice in front of a mirror for five minutes while trying to look as crazy as possible. Decide whether that's the way you look when you are outside.

- If you fear blushing, use blush or other means to make yourself look very flushed.

- If you fear sweating in front of others, apply drops of water onto your forehead and wet your armpits to look as if you were sweating.

- If you are very fearful of showing imperfection because you may be judged adversely, make a mistake on purpose.

- With a dentist or hairdresser, work with someone who is understanding. Tell the person that you are nervous. Plan to have a small job done first.

- Plan to ask for a short rest room or coffee break when one is not offered (allowing you to feel in charge of the situation).

- If your fear of negative judgement is particularly disturbing to you and you would like more guidance, we recommend the book *Dying of Embarrassment* (Markway et al. 1992).

Walking Outside

Fear of walking outside is usually related to a fear of a symptom attack. Sometimes it is part of space phobia (see chapter 2). If you fear walking outside alone, you need to practice on it *daily*.

Suggestions on Exposure Planning

- Walk around the block. As soon as you can, do so without safety devices such as a cell phone.

- Walk around the same block, repeating about three to four loops.

- Walk around two to three blocks with repeated loops.

- Walk away from home for fifteen minutes and back.

- Walk away from home for thirty minutes and back.

- Drive somewhere and take a longer walk, around a lake, in a neighborhood, or around a park.

APPENDIX F

Worksheets

All the worksheets are repeated in this appendix. Right before you start with chapter 1, we strongly urge you to make copies of these worksheets. The worksheets are there for you to practice on and learn from, so don't be stingy making copies. If you want to save paper, you can make two-sided copies. Having worksheets handy will increase the chances that you will actually work with them. Below is a suggestion on how many copies you will need of each one. Please make these copies and have them handy before starting with chapter 1. You can make more copies later, if necessary.

Number of Copies You Need to Make of Each Worksheet:

Worksheet 1: How Catastrophic Thinking and Avoidant Coping Fuel Your Phobia   —**1**

Worksheet 2: Your Goals and Objectives   —**1**

Worksheet 3: Challenging Felt Beliefs   —**10**

Worksheet 4: Your Daily Interoceptive Exposure Log   —**2 to 4**

Worksheet 5: Your Situational Fear Hierarchy   —**2**

Worksheet 6: Your Weekly Situational Exposure Log   —**10 or more**

Worksheet 7: Maintenance Exposures Log   —**4**

Worksheet 1: How Catastrophic Thinking and Avoidant Coping Fuel Your Phobia

Danger signals
(What internal sensations
in what external situation?)
↓

1) Describe one combination of danger
signals (at least one internal and one
external) that makes you anxious: _____

_____

_____

↓

*Misinterpretation of the
danger signal*
↓

2) Why is that combination of danger
signals dangerous? What symptom attack
and catastrophe might it lead to? _____

_____

_____

↓

Emotional response
(anxiety, panic)
↓

3) What emotion do you experience
when in the presence of this combination
of danger signals? _____

_____

↓

Avoidant coping
↓

4) List the ways in which you try to
avoid the symptom attack and the feared
catastrophe: _____

_____

_____

_____

_____

↓

*Absence of a corrective
experience*
(No new learning takes
place on an emotional level.)

5) How has your avoidance interfered
with learning? (What do you still need to
learn in order to feel different about the
danger signals?) _____

_____

Worksheet 2: Your Goals and Objectives

List your goals and objectives below.   *Check them off as you achieve them.*

Goal # _____ :

_____ ☐

Objectives:

_____ ☐

_____ ☐

_____ ☐

_____ ☐

_____ ☐

_____ ☐

_____ ☐

Goal # _____ :

_____ ☐

Objectives:

_____ ☐

_____ ☐

_____ ☐

_____ ☐

_____ ☐

_____ ☐

_____ ☐

Worksheet 3:
Challenging Felt Beliefs

1. **Date:**

2. **External Danger Signal** (Write down the specific situation that makes you anxious):

3. **Internal Danger Signal** (Write down the specific sensations that make you anxious):

4. **Feared Symptom Attack** (If panic, specify what sensations in the panic scare you):

5. **Feared Catastrophe** (Write down the exact thing, i.e., the worst thing, that you think will happen):

6. **Challenging the Threat**

Your evidence: Why you think the catastrophic fear will happen; does not have to be logical.

Then refute! Counter your evidence using your own or other people's past experience or logic.

Alternatives: Can the sensations/the event have another explanation or lead to something harmless?

So, what if? If your fear is social threat, and you truly were rejected, what would happen?

Worksheet 4:
Your Daily Interoceptive Exposure Log

Sensations you are provoking: _____

_____

_____

Sensation Intensity = Highest level of sensation intensity during exercise (0=lowest to 10=highest)

Anxiety Level = Highest level of anxiety/fear during exercise (0=lowest to 10=highest)

Day of Week/ Date	Name of exercise and where you are doing it	Length of Time	Sensation Intensity (0–10)	Anxiety Level (0–10)

Worksheet 5: Your Situational Fear Hierarchy

Low-Challenge Exposures (Anxiety Levels 1–3):

_____

_____

_____

_____

_____

_____

Medium-Challenge Exposures (Anxiety Levels 4–6):

_____

_____

_____

_____

_____

_____

High-Challenge Exposures (Anxiety Levels 7–10):

_____

_____

_____

_____

_____

_____

Worksheet 6:
Your Weekly Situational Exposure Log

Exposures planned for the week starting _____ :

_____

_____

_____

Exposures Accomplished:

Day of Week/ Date	External Situation (Add distance/time)	Interoceptive Exercise (Done during or right before)	Anxiety Level (0–10) Peak	End
Mon				
Tues				
Wed				
Thur				
Fri				
Sat				
Sun				

Did you achieve your plan for the week? _____ Yes _____ No
(If not entirely, are there any modifications you need to make to improve the success of next week's plan?)

Worksheet 7: Maintenance Exposures Log

Day of Week/Date	Continued Exposures (Add Distance/Time)

References

American Psychiatric Association. 2000. *Diagnostic and Statistical Manual of Mental Disorders, Fourth Edition. Text Revision.* Washington, D.C.: American Psychiatric Association.

Amering, M., H. Katschnig, P. Berger, J. Windhaber, W. Baischer, and K. Dantendorfer. 1997. Embarrassment about the first panic attack predicts agoraphobia in panic disorder patients. *Behaviour Research and Therapy* 35(6):517–521.

Barlow, D. H. 1988. *Anxiety and Its Disorders: The Nature and Treatment of Anxiety and Panic.* New York: The Guilford Press.

Barlow, D. H., and M. G. Craske. 1994. *Mastery of Your Anxiety and Panic II.* San Antonio: Graywind Publications/The Psychological Corporation.

Brandt, T. 1996. Phobic postural vertigo. *Neurology* 46:1515–1519.

Brown, D. 1996. *Flying without Fear.* Oakland, Calif.: New Harbinger Publications.

Craske, M. G., M. Rowe, M. Lewin, and R. Noriega-Dimitri. 1997. Interoceptive exposure versus breathing retraining in cognitive-behavioural therapy for panic disorder with agoraphobia. *British Journal of Clinical Psychology* 36:85–99.

Davis, Martha, Elizabeth Robbins Eshelman, and Matthew McKay. 2000. *The Relaxation & Stress Reduction Wrokbook, Fifth edition.* Oakland, Calif.: New Harbinger Publications.

Drummond, L. M. 1993. Behavioural approaches to anxiety disorders. *Postgraduate Medical Journal* 69(8):222–226.

Epstein, S. 1993. *You're Smarter Than You Think.* New York: Simon and Schuster.

Fava, G. A., G. Savron, M. Zielezny, S. Grandi, C. Rafanelli, and S. Conti. 1997. Overcoming resistance to exposure in panic disorder with agoraphobia. *Acta Psychiatrica Scandinavica* 95:306–312.

Hahlweg, K., W. Fiegenbaum, M. Frank, B. Schroeder, and I. von Witzleben. 2001. Short- and long-term effectiveness of an empirically supported treatment for agoraphobia. *Journal of Counseling and Clinical Psychology* 69(3):375–382.

Kabat-Zinn, J. 1990. *Full Catastrophe Living: Using the Wisdom of Your Body and Mind to Face Stress, Pain, and Illness.* New York: Dell Publishing.

———. 1994. *Wherever You Go, There You Are: Mindfulness Meditation in Everyday Life.* New York: Hyperion.

Klerman, G. L. 1992. Treatments for panic disorder. *Journal of Clinical Psychiatry* 53(3)Suppl.:14–19.

Lelliott, P., I. Marks, G. McNamee, and A. Tobeña. 1989. Onset of panic disorder with agoraphobia: Toward an integrated model. *Archives of General Psychiatry* 46:1000–1004.

Marks, I., and R. Dar. 2000. Fear reduction by psychotherapies: A response. *British Journal of Psychiatry* 177:280.

Markway, B. G., C. N. Carmin, C. A. Pollard, and T. Flynn. 1992. *Dying of Embarrassment.* Oakland, Calif.: New Harbinger Publications.

McCaffrey, R. J., R. M. Rapee, D. A. Gansler, and D. H. Barlow. 1990. Interaction of neuropsychological and psychological factors in two cases of "space phobia." *Journal of Behavior Therapy and Experimental Psychiatry* 21(2):113–120.

Öhman, A., and S. Mineka. 2001. Fears, phobias, and preparedness: Toward an evolved module of fear and fear learning. *Psychological Review* 108(3):483–522.

Pollard, C. A., R. C. Tait, D. Meldrum, I. H. Dubinsky, and J. S. Gall. 1996. Agoraphobia without panic: Case illustrations of an overlooked syndrome. *Journal of Nervous and Mental Disease* 184(1):61–62.

Tilton, R. 2000. Lecture delivered at the Conference of the Anxiety Disorders Association of America, Cognitive Therapy Center, Riverside, Calif.

Westphal, C. F. 1988. *Die Agoraphobia.* Translated by T. J. Knapp and M. T. Shumacker. Lahman, Maryland: University Press of America.

World Health Organization. 1992. *International Classification of Diseases and Related Health Problems, Tenth Revision.* Geneva: World Health Organization.

Zuercher-White, E. 1997. *Treating Panic Disorder and Agoraphobia: A Step-by-Step Clinical Guide.* Oakland, Calif.: New Harbinger Publications.

————. 1998. *An End to Panic: Breakthrough Techniques for Overcoming Panic Disorder.* Oakland, Calif.: New Harbinger Publications.

Some Other
New Harbinger Titles

Freeing the Angry Mind, Item 4380 $14.95

Living Beyond Your Pain, Item 4097 $19.95

Transforming Anxiety, Item 4445 $12.95

Integrative Treatment for Borderline Personality Disorder, Item 4461 $24.95

Depressed and Anxious, Item 3635 $19.95

Is He Depressed or What?, Item 4240 $15.95

Cognitive Therapy for Obsessive-Compulsive Disorder, Item 4291 $39.95

Child and Adolescent Psychopharmacology Made Simple, Item 4356 $14.95

ACT* on Life Not on Anger, Item 4402 $14.95

Overcoming Medical Phobias, Item 3872 $14.95

Acceptance & Commitment Therapy for Anxiety Disorders, Item 4275 $58.95

The OCD Workbook, Item 4224 $19.95

Neural Path Therapy, Item 4267 $14.95

Overcoming Obsessive Thoughts, Item 3813 $14.95

The Interpersonal Solution to Depression, Item 4186 $19.95

Get Out of Your Mind & Into Your Life, Item 4259 $19.95

Dialectical Behavior Therapy in Private Practice, Item 4208 $54.95

The Anxiety & Phobia Workbook, 4th edition, Item 4135 $19.95

Loving Someone with OCD, Item 3295 $15.95

Overcoming Animal & Insect Phobias, Item 3880 $12.95

Overcoming Compulsive Washing, Item 4054 $14.95

Angry All the Time, Item 3929 $13.95

Handbook of Clinical Psychopharmacology for Therapists, 4th edition, Item 3996 $55.95

Writing For Emotional Balance, Item 3821 $14.95

Surviving Your Borderline Parent, Item 3287 $14.95

When Anger Hurts, 2nd edition, Item 3449 $16.95

Calming Your Anxious Mind, Item 3384 $12.95

Ending the Depression Cycle, Item 3333 $17.95

Your Surviving Spirit, Item 3570 $18.95

Coping with Anxiety, Item 3201 $10.95

The Agoraphobia Workbook, Item 3236 $19.95

Loving the Self-Absorbed, Item 3546 $14.95

Transforming Anger, Item 352X $12.95

Don't Let Your Emotions Run Your Life, Item 3090 $18.95

Made in the USA
Columbia, SC
04 June 2021